"Andy Paul obliterates outdated legacy approaches to sales, the revolting behaviors that repel buyers. He replaces them with the most human of attributes and strategies that will accelerate your clients' decisions and your results. Death to salesy!"
ANTHONY IANNARINO, author of *Elite Sales Strategies*

"Andy Paul's new book is a must-read not just for frontline salespeople but for all of us to rethink and reconfigure how we connect, communicate, and persuade."
DREW NEISSER, founder of Renegade and CMO Huddles and author of *Renegade Marketing*

"Andy Paul reminds us that sales remains a human business, and he provides a behavioral roadmap for increasing our ability to connect in sales and other situations. Rooted in decades of experience and deep knowledge about buying behaviors, *Sell Without Selling Out* makes crucial distinctions—influence versus persuasion, understanding versus knowing your customer, listening versus hearing, being responsive versus being fast—that drive success in selling and in life."
FRANK CESPEDES, senior lecturer at Harvard Business School and author of *Sales Management That Works*

"Andy Paul nails it! To sell is human; to buy is human. It is at this human-to-human intersection that top sales professionals shine."
JEB BLOUNT, CEO of Sales Gravy and author of *Sales EQ*

"Increasing your sales without losing your soul can feel impossible. But as you'll discover in *Sell Without Selling Out*, there are simple paths to gain your buyers' attention and make sense of the often contradictory information available today. In a world of bots and automation, *Sell Without Selling Out* is a must-read for individuals and team leaders who know that to sell more, you must first be more."
SHARI LEVITIN, bestselling author of *Heart and Sell*

"It's a truism that people don't like being sold to. Very few sales authors have written about the tragically self-centered approach taken by most sales processes and salespeople. But no one has addressed it so directly and thoroughly. Andy Paul takes down the Selling Out mentality that is so dominant in the profession and constructively replaces it with the human alternative, Selling In. This book doesn't just tear things down, it helps you build them back up—from a place you already know is right for you and your customers. *Sell Without Selling Out* is a must-read for all sales professionals."
CHARLES GREEN, co-author of *The Trusted Advisor* and author of *Trust-Based Selling*

"*Sell Without Selling Out* helps rescue the sales profession from misguided and wrongheaded stereotypes. With both savvy and humanity, Andy Paul lays out the simple steps all salespeople can take to become the best version of themselves."
DANIEL H. PINK, #1 *New York Times* bestselling author of *To Sell Is Human, When*, and *Drive*

"This book captures exactly how selling can be a noble profession in which we make a positive difference in the lives of others with integrity and positive influence. Every leader should read Andy Paul's book and find ways to enshrine its content in the hearts and minds of their salespeople. *Sell Without Selling Out* is a timeless masterpiece on which you can build a brilliant and lasting career and business."

TONY HUGHES, bestselling author and speaker on sales leadership

"As a customer, what more could you hope for in a salesperson than someone who takes the time to connect with you as a human and is curious about your life, challenges, and vision for success? Someone who quickly understands exactly where you're trying to make progress and why you're stuck? If they generously helped you succeed and navigate along the way, you'd be blown away! That's how I felt reading this book, and that's what this book can help you learn as a seller. Simple to read, easy to absorb, timeless but urgent. Your customers and career will thank you."

ANDREW SYKES, founder and CEO of Habits at Work

"Andy Paul has given us a breath of fresh air with this book. His four Sell In Pillars are a recipe for authentic selling and taking control of how to serve the marketplace. Applying what you learn here will elevate the brand and reputation of our beloved sales profession. Sell In!"

RALPH BARSI, sales leader and advisor

"*Sell Without Selling Out* will turn everything you knew about selling upside down. And it's about time! Customers are increasingly doing everything they can to minimize the need to engage salespeople in their buying journeys. Andy Paul shows how salespeople continue to do the opposite of what customers really want and need, focusing on their selling objectives and not on what would be most helpful to the customer. Andy reminds us that buying and selling are human processes, and common sense. Andy's book will change the way you sell—and your customers will demonstrate their appreciation by actively engaging you in their buying processes. Thanks for helping us get back to the core principles we seem to have lost, Andy!"
DAVID BROCK, CEO of Partners In EXCELLENCE and author of *Sales Manager Survival Guide*

"Most sales books teach worn-out techniques and tactics. *Sell Without Selling Out* provides a refreshing and practical guide to what it means to be a modern seller. It starts with being a good human. The core pillars of Connection, Curiosity, Understanding, and Generosity are what separate open-minded professional sellers from salesy closers. A must-read for individual contributors and leaders."
BRANDON FLUHARTY, vice president of strategic account solutions at LivePerson and founder of Be Focused. Live Great.

● PAGE
● TWO

SELL

WITHOUT SELLING OUT

A Guide to Success
on Your Own Terms

ANDY PAUL

Cataloguing in publication information is available from Library and Archives Canada.
ISBN 978-1-989603-57-4 (paperback)
ISBN 978-1-77458-088-2 (ebook)
ISBN 978-1-77458-173-5 (audiobook)

Page Two
pagetwo.com

Edited by Amanda Lewis
Copyedited by Rachel Ironstone
Cover and interior design by Jennifer Lum
Printed and bound in Canada by Friesens
Distributed in Canada by Raincoast Books
Distributed in the US and internationally by Macmillan Publishers

22 23 24 25 26   5 4 3 2 1

andypaul.com

TO VICKY.

Of course, none of this would have been possible without you. I'm in constant awe of the profound impact you've had on the lives of your students. If this book can have even a fraction of that impact on the careers of the people who read it, then it will be an amazing success.

"Insist on yourself;
never imitate."

RALPH WALDO EMERSON

CONTENTS

AUTHOR'S NOTE

THIS BOOK IS not another work of fiction about how you can morph overnight into a sales superstar. There's none of that BS here.

This book is about making the choice to turn your back on the salesy behaviors that are so embedded in modern sales. Behaviors that make everyone cringe, including you. That's the Selling Out part.

It's about learning how to become consistently proficient at selling simply by understanding what's most important to your buyers. And then helping them get it. That's the Selling In part.

Perhaps most importantly, this book is about learning how to experience the energy, impact, and fulfillment that come from being the best version of yourself in any sales situation.

You're going to like *Sell Without Selling Out*. It's full of road-tested ideas that you can quickly and easily put to use in your selling today. Start with just one, something that will make a difference.

I LOVE YOU, YOU'RE PERFECT, NOW CHANGE

IMAGINE THAT YOU'RE unattached and looking for a romantic partner.

You meet someone at a party at a friend's house. They have a certain something about them—smart and stylish, they have a quality that appears to make everything look easy for them. Upon first meeting, you think this person possesses a lot of the qualities you've been seeking in a partner. It turns out the attraction is mutual. You start a relationship.

However, as you begin to spend more time together, it becomes apparent that this new partner, while outwardly attractive, doesn't share your basic core values. Or your outlook on life. They aren't curious about the world. They aren't really interested in anyone but themself. They ask only superficial questions about you and your day. When you have a difference of opinion, they assume they know what's bothering you and don't make a sincere effort to really understand your concerns. You're starting to wonder whether they are trustworthy or reliable.

You're having doubts. You're very attracted to this person. If you could just be together without having to ever talk, it might work.

What the hell are you thinking? As much fun as it is to be with this person, you're not making progress. They clearly aren't able to provide you the support you need to achieve your life goals.

You have a choice to make.

Now imagine this partner is your sales process.

The methods and processes that sales bosses want you to follow are all superficially attractive. The practice of sales—the way you've been trained, the methods and techniques you've been taught, the content you consume online about how to sell—make everything look so easy.

Do this to 10X your sales.

Say these three words at this time in a sales conversation and you're guaranteed to 5X your conversions.

Blah.

Blah.

Blah.

It's all very attractive, but it's not connected to reality. It doesn't sync with who you are as a person, and it's not aligned with how you want to help your buyers achieve their goals. And it's definitely not aligned with how your buyers make their decisions.

So, if these things don't feel right to you, in your gut, why are you doing them?

I call that Selling Out: choosing to sell in a way that is not aligned with who you are and what your buyers want you to be. What they need you to be. In short, being "salesy."

Look, being in sales is hard enough. It's a tough job, a lonely job. You're on an island all by yourself with your monthly number. Why make it harder by selling in a way that turns you into someone you don't recognize?

You have a choice. Sell out your future, your values, and yourself for possible short-term gain. Or stay true to yourself and create success on your own terms. I call that Selling In. Selling In aligns how you sell with who you are as a person. And it aligns with how your buyer wants to work with a seller. Selling In allows you to become the best version of yourself.

After a brief foray into Selling Out when I first started selling, I shifted into Selling In and have had an incredibly fulfilling and rewarding career in sales.

I received an excellent early sales and business education by selling computer and software systems to midsize businesses in the Bay Area. There was no better learning experience at the start of a sales career than being able to chat with successful entrepreneurs about how they built their businesses and how I could help them achieve their next level of growth and profitability.

I grew from that beginning into positions where I sold hundreds of millions of dollars' worth of complex communications products and services to very large enterprises around the globe. For years I lived on airplanes, winning big deals on every continent but Antarctica.

I've grown sales teams at successful start-ups (and some that weren't so successful).

I've run my own sales consulting business for twenty years, helping companies turn around under-performing sales teams. I've published two previous sales books, and I created and host the influential *Sales Enablement Podcast with Andy Paul*, featuring more than a thousand conversations with some of the best and brightest minds in the industry. In 2020 I sold my podcast to ringDNA, a high-growth SaaS (software as a service) start-up.

Any success I've achieved I attribute to one decision I made at the very beginning of my sales career: I was determined to act and sell in a way that aligned with who I am as a person, my values and character. I didn't see a choice. Otherwise, it was going to be a very short career.

Have I been perfect in this regard? God, no. But the times when I had to sell out, to act with a buyer in a manner that made both of us uncomfortable, thankfully were so few that they are still burned into my memory. (Jack, my apologies for calling you in the middle of Christmas Eve Mass to ask you to fax that order to me. They made me do it.)

Selling Out is surrender. It's giving in to ways of selling that are out of alignment with who you are as a person. Selling In is embracing behaviors that are in alignment with your values and with what your buyers need from you.

➡ **What we do**, as sellers, isn't complicated. We listen to understand what the most important thing is to our buyers. And then we help them get it.

The legendary sales trainer Zig Ziglar once said, "You will get all you want in life, if you help enough other people get what they want." This book is about how you do that in a way that best aligns with how your buyers want to work with you. And, as importantly, in a way that's aligned with how you want to act as a person.

It starts by laying out how traditional sales behaviors work against you and against what you're trying to accomplish in sales. And in life. I'll teach you how to take control of how you sell in order to help your buyer achieve the thing that's most important to them, and help you achieve what's most important to you. All on your own terms.

At the heart of taking control are four core sales behaviors. These are the Sell In Pillars: Connection, Curiosity, Understanding, Generosity. Everything that I've accomplished in my professional and personal lives has stemmed from how I've embodied these four behaviors to help others achieve the things that are most important to them. Everything else is window dressing.

In this book, you'll learn how to embrace these pillars and use them to become the very best sales version of yourself.

Finally, I'll show you how to use Selling In to shorten the buyer's journey and accelerate your sales. The method will surprise you with its simplicity and effectiveness.

Selling In clicks because it is natural, innate human behavior. We are wired to connect, to be curious, to understand, and to be generous. Being human is the shortest path to helping your buyers get what is most important to them.

Selling Out is the opposite of natural. Like food dye Red No. 2. Or a badly fitted toupee that's perched on a man's head like a small rodent waiting to pounce. Selling Out is learned behavior. That's why it's awkward and soulless. That's why it doesn't feel right to your buyers or to you. It's the shortest path to burnout (and a career change).

In his book about the future of work, *Humans Are Underrated*, Geoff Colvin wrote that success in the future will belong to those people who learn how to become "more intensely human." Meaning that the high achievers will be the people who learn how to be really proficient at those human behaviors that machines can't replicate well. That's Selling In.

Selling Out could easily be automated using today's technologies. Repetitive sales actions that have no value for the buyer are prime candidates for becoming the province of the machines.

Sell in or sell out. The choice is up to you. Make yours by reading on.

CHAPTER

1

WHAT HUMAN BEING ACTS THIS WAY?

MY FIRST SALES training class took place in the basement of a Holiday Inn in Pasadena, California, a block from the route of the annual New Year's Day Rose Parade. I sat in a darkened room with thirty other newbie salespeople, watching a video of a creepily sincere, slick-haired con man. This top trainer, with a demeanor reminiscent of an early Sunday morning TV preacher, was teaching us how to sell.

How to open a conversation with a phony icebreaker.

How to bully through objections.

How to trial close with misdirection.

How to use persuasion to hammer the prospect into submission.

At the time, this behavior was considered state-of-the-art sales technique.

It made my skin crawl.

I asked myself, "What human being acts this way?"

Unfortunately, mainstream sales methods haven't progressed much since then.

This training class took place during my third week on the job for Burroughs Corp, at the time the number two computer company in the world. It was my very first sales job. In my first two weeks, before heading off to training, I'd tagged along on sales calls with several of the senior sellers from my branch office in Oakland. And from those few ride-alongs, I'd already developed a persistent sense of dread—let's go ahead and call it impending doom—about what I would face after I returned from my initial sales training.

In my training class there were new Burroughs sales reps from all over the country. There were lots of false smiles and really firm handshakes on the morning of the first class. As we went around the room and introduced ourselves, some reps humble-bragged about all the cold calls they'd already made. Others went into detail about the deals they'd closed in their first weeks on the job. Cold calls? Closed deals? I felt sick to my stomach. Was I falling behind already?

On top of everything else, there was something off about nearly every person in my class. At first I couldn't put my finger on it. Then it hit me. Everyone was trying so hard to be ... salesy. It was if they had all put on a uniform that required them to act the part of a prototypical perky, pushy salesperson.

I couldn't be that person.

At least outwardly, I was the least salesy person in the room. I was shy and self-conscious in group settings. The role-plays we did in class were mortifying. It wasn't just that I was introverted. I was so far out of my comfort zone that I'd completely forgotten where I misplaced it.

In less than two weeks, I'd be back in my branch office, driving out into the field by 8:30 every morning to make dozens of cold calls on unsuspecting buyers who, as regular human beings, instinctively recoiled in the face of the cringe-inducing sales methods I'd just learned.

And that, in a nutshell, was my problem. I just couldn't be that person. I *wouldn't* be that person.

In order to sell, would I have to become a sellout? I felt the conflict that nearly every seller feels at multiple points in their career. To do this job, would I have to become someone I wouldn't recognize when I looked at myself in the mirror?

CHAPTER 2

STAND OUT
OR SELL OUT

I N *ATOMIC HABITS*, author James Clear writes, "Every action is a vote for the type of person you wish to become." This statement begs the question: what type of seller do you want to become? A sellout who struggles to establish a firm footing in sales? Or a consistently good seller who sells in and stands out year after year?

There's often a yawning chasm between how sellers imagine themselves professionally interacting with and helping their buyers, and how they sell in reality. There's also a wide gap between how their buyer perceives them and how they would like to be perceived, which is as a trusted advisor and source of value.

Pushy. Self-interested. Lazy. Uninformed. Clueless. Buyers often use these adjectives to describe salespeople.

Unfair? Of course. But buyers' seemingly instinctive distrust of sellers didn't materialize out of thin air. Buyers' experiences with sellers continue to reinforce this negative perception. And sellers have helped perpetuate this problem through the salesy techniques and behaviors they're trained to use.

It doesn't need to be this way. But the impetus for change has to come from you, the individual seller. It's not going to come from your bosses or managers. They're invested in the status quo.

So, let's assess where you currently are on your Selling In journey. Take a look at this chart of individual sales mindsets and attributes and see which column most closely resembles where you are now.

SELLING OUT	SELLING IN
Pitch	Conversation
Tell	Ask questions
Persuasion	Influence
Change minds	Help make up minds
Taker	Giver
Transaction	Transformation
Stays on-script	Curious
Knowledge	Understanding
Listen to respond	Listen to understand
Know-it-all	Learn-it-all

Prioritize orders	Prioritize outcomes
Product pusher	Problem solver
Process	People
Sells products (drills)	Sells outcomes (holes)
What's important to me?	What's important to the buyer?
Know what's best for buyer	Help buyer understand what's best
Salesy	Open-minded
Low win rate	High win rate
Closer	Seller
It's all about me	I win when the buyer wins
Extract value	Give value
Sales process	Buying process

Selling Out and Selling In sit on the opposite ends of a spectrum. Where do you currently sit?

SELLING OUT_____ SELLING IN

Now, what would it take to move you more toward Selling In?

You get to decide which actions will enable you to become the type of seller you want to be: one who actually helps the buyer, or one who pushes a product or service on the buyer in a way that leaves both of you feeling dirty and a bit ashamed to make eye contact.

You can become the standout seller who doesn't have to sell out to get what you want out of your sales career.

CHAPTER

3

SELLING TO HUMANS

WHAT YOUR BUYERS NEED FROM YOU

SALES IS A human business. So, I really hate to say this, but...

Sellers aren't very good at selling to humans.

More often than not, your customers make the decision to buy from you *in spite of you*, not because of you.

If you're going to stop Selling Out, you have to take control of how you sell. Before you can do that, you first have to understand exactly what your buyers need from you.

According to a Forrester study, executives consider less than one fifth of the meetings they have with salespeople to be valuable.[1] In other words, more than 80 percent of buyers earned zero return on the time and attention they invested in you.

Buyers are figuratively holding their noses and buying from you in spite of your best efforts to sell to them. This happens primarily because you have been Selling Out.

Look at selling this way: every choice and decision a buyer makes during their buying journey is their referendum on you. And it's personal. Not in a "you're a bad human" sort of a way. Personal as in "you don't really understand what's most important to me, so I don't have confidence that you can help me get it."

If, to paraphrase Dan Pink, to sell is human, then we need to learn how to get much better at selling to humans. Because our buyers are moving on without us.

In its 2018 research on buyer enablement, Gartner® mapped out an intricate flow-diagram that charted the steps of the B2B (business-to-business) buyer's purchasing journey.[2]

In this densely packed flow chart, the word *sales* is mentioned only once. Ouch! The message from B2B buyers is clear: you, the sellers, aren't providing us, the buyers, with enough value to help us make a decision, so we'll have to figure out this whole thing on our own. (Cue the analyst reports that breathlessly predict the looming obsolescence of B2B sales jobs.)

It doesn't have to be that way. It really doesn't.

You see, buyers want your help. They need your help.

They need *you*. The human seller. It's true.

I know, you've read the results of surveys with buyers that were published during the COVID-19 pandemic that confidently stated that the world had changed, that B2B buyers really don't want to engage with salespeople.

Well, talk about old news. No buyer in the history of B2B selling, or maybe in the entire history of civilization, has ever wanted to talk with a salesperson. I'm very good at what I do, but my customers aren't waiting for me to call them for a friendly chat. We're not trying to make friends with our buyers. We're working to help them solve their problems to achieve the business outcomes that are most important to them.

When your buyers set out to explore the purchase of a new product or service, what is their mindset?

Do they want to invest unlimited amounts of time and effort to exhaustively investigate all their alternatives? I mean, if they've recognized that they have a problem to solve, or a pain point to cure, do they dismiss the urgency and give themselves as much time as they need to make the optimal decision?

No.

So when a buyer is ready to have a conversation with you, when a buyer is prepared to invest their time and attention in you, it's because they need your help. They've gone as far as they can go on their own, and now they've turned to you.

At that moment your buyer needs your help to a) quickly gather and make sense of the information they need to make a decision about how to get their most important thing and b) accomplish this with the least possible investment of their time, attention, and resources.

Your job as a seller is to listen to understand what the most important thing is to your buyer. And then help them get it.

Your buyers need your help with that second part; the "help them get it" part.

This means that your buyers need your help to quickly gather and make sense of the information they need to make their decision with the least possible investment of their time, attention, and resources.

But here's the thing. Selling Out doesn't get them there. Buyers don't need your process. They don't need a dose of your earnest persuasion. They don't need you to be salesy. They'll go through their buyer's journey without you if you add friction to their process and force them to invest more time and attention than necessary.

If you start Selling In, every sales action you take will align with this goal of your buyers. They need your influence to help them make the right choices and decisions. Start Selling In and you'll become the reason your buyers decide to buy from your company. Not your product. Not your company. You.

➡ Your buyers need your help to quickly gather and make sense of the information they need to make their decision with the **least possible investment of their time**, attention, and resources.

CHAPTER
4

YOU'RE NOT THE BOSS OF ME

SEIZE CONTROL OF HOW YOU SELL

S TEP ONE IN your transformation from Selling Out to Selling In starts with taking control of how you sell.

That's why your sales boss will hate that you're reading this book. Selling In requires that you behave more independently, act more autonomously, and exert more personal control over how you sell.

Sellers largely operate in environments in which too many sales bosses prioritize conformity and predictable mediocrity (or is it mediocre predictability?). They slap a few layers of new technology on outmoded sales processes and call them "modern." Sales processes that are enforced by data-driven metrics and key performance indicators (KPIs) rob sellers of their autonomy and strip the soul out of selling.

But sales bosses are afraid to stray from what they know, afraid to stray from the playbook that sort of works. Adopting a sales approach that differs too much from the herd mentality, even if it makes sense, could be disruptive to their careers.

However, that's their problem. Not yours. You have to do what is best for your buyers. Just so I'm clear: what's best for your buyers is also what's best for you.

Socrates wrote, "To find yourself, think for yourself."

Taking control starts by thinking for yourself.

Perhaps because I'm a child of the sixties, I question everything—much to the dismay of bosses throughout my career. I never saw the upside of blind obedience to whatever sales process or sales methodology was imposed on me. Instead, what interested me was learning those things that were going to give me the highest probability of success when I interacted with my buyers. Those insights came from customers, peers, books, and, occasionally, my bosses.

I was fortunate to have a couple of patient and supportive managers along the way who encouraged me to define my own path. Of course, there were also sales bosses who were control freaks and weren't too happy that I generally ignored their direction. And you know what? It didn't matter because I delivered.

One executive VP grew a little agitated after we'd worked together for about a year. Over the course of that year, every time he gave me some sales advice or a suggestion, I'd give some variation of my normal response: "That's interesting. Let me think about that."

I'd consider whether his suggestion aligned with my sales process and would add value to help me move the deal forward. I know it frustrated him because like most bosses he just wanted me to accept his advice and act on it. But it was my butt on the line, not his. If I was going to lose an opportunity, I wanted it to be due to decisions I made and actions I took. I was perfectly prepared to be held accountable for that.

Finally, one day after he'd given me a suggestion and I'd responded that I'd think about it, he threw up his hands and said, "Do you ever just say yes to something?"

To which I replied... well, you know.

No one cares about your success as much as you do. You have to look at your career this way. Bosses can order you to follow their suggestions, but if you do that and don't hit your numbers, they could fire you. They don't care that you were acting on their orders.

Don't blindly follow a boss's sales advice if it means Selling Out. That will never be good for your buyer. Or you. Think for yourself. Accept the advice that will help you be the seller you want to become. Politely decline the rest.

That's how I did it. This meant that I had to constantly learn, expriment, change, and adapt to new situations. I was continually pushing myself out of my comfort zone to broaden my knowledge and capabilities.

It was risky. I built on my experience, listened to my gut, gathered ideas from various sources, and then made a decision about what would work best. I didn't substitute someone else's judgment for my own. I was responsible.

If I was going to fail, it was going to be on my own terms. And when I succeeded, the satisfaction I felt from doing it my way, and my motivation to keep improving, skyrocketed.

You're going to be confronted with a similar choice more than once in your career. You can stick with the "authorized" way of selling. Or you can pick and choose the parts that work for you, add what you learn through your experiences, and develop a more effective and productive personal sales process that is aligned with your unique strengths and your buyers' needs.

Francesca Gino of Harvard Business School writes about the importance of blazing your own path. In a recent article, she indicates that research shows "going against the crowd gives us confidence in our actions, which makes us feel unique and engaged and translates to higher performance and greater creativity."[3] That's the value you receive from taking control of how you sell.

It takes courage to stand up to the status quo, and your bosses, and commit to selling your way. But take a cue from Glennon Doyle, who wrote in her memoir, *Untamed*: "Brave means living from the inside out."

Selling In means to sell from the inside out. Here are some ideas on how to be brave:

- **Don't compromise:** When I was young my dad would tell me, "At the end of our lives, the only thing people will remember of us is our character." Don't do anything that would force you to compromise your values, ethics, or integrity.

- **Experiment more:** Constantly experiment in order to improve every aspect of your selling. Clint Dempsey was one of the greatest American soccer players. When asked what made Dempsey so good, his former coach, Bruce Arena, simply said, "He tries shit." There's no rule book for sales. *Try shit.*

- **Develop your team:** Being in control doesn't mean you know everything. And it doesn't mean you don't need help. Develop a team who can provide you unfiltered coaching, advice, and support when you need it. Your team can include your boss, a mentor, a peer from inside or outside your company, or even a customer— whomever you trust to be truthful with you.

Remember, you like working in sales. You want to find fulfillment in your work, and you want to develop financial security to support yourself and your family. You know you can achieve more in sales than you have so far.

But that can only happen if you stop Selling Out and are prepared to take complete responsibility for how you sell.

CHAPTER

5

DEATH TO SALESY

THE NEXT STEP in taking control of how you sell is to refuse to act in ways that buyers automatically resist. Here's the thing. Selling is very simple.

Don't confuse simple with easy. Selling is hard, hard work. That is never going to change. But, c'mon, sellers make selling unnecessarily hard by acting in ways that turn off their buyers. It doesn't have to be that way.

Let me keep it real simple for you. Stop acting salesy. Your buyer doesn't like it. You don't like it. Stop it.

Let me illustrate why salesy needs to go. The one question I guarantee that your buyers will never ask you is, "Could you be more salesy?" As in, "Andy, we'd like to buy your product, but we feel that you're just not salesy enough for us. Could you be more salesy?"

That would never happen. Yet sellers persist.

Let's look at *salesy* from the buyer's perspective. Being salesy is a way of acting that universally makes buyers squirm. Salesy is Selling Out.

Ask yourself this question: Is "being more salesy" the answer to helping my buyer

- define the problem they need to solve,
- make sense of the information that I provide,
- understand their options for achieving their most important thing,
- calculate the value of my solution, or
- make an informed decision?

The answer is a resounding NO.

Similarly, ask yourself the following questions around sales challenges you may face and consider whether "Be more salesy" is the answer to helping with any one of them.

- How do I close more deals?
- How do I increase my win rate?
- How do I build a better connection with a buyer?
- How do I demonstrate my credibility to a buyer?
- How do I earn the trust of a buyer?
- How do I conduct a better discovery call?
- How do I discover my buyer's most important thing?
- How do I handle objections?
- How do I do a better demo?
- How do I effectively qualify my prospects?
- How do I give good value to the buyer?

Is being more salesy the right approach? Again, the answer is a deafening NO.

So if being more salesy isn't the answer to anything useful, why do you do it?

Perhaps it's how you've been trained. The vast majority of sales training is designed to teach sellers like you how to be more salesy.

To make it worse, sales bosses reinforce the idea of being salesy with how they coach and manage you. It's not really their fault. They're just repeating the behaviors that they believed worked for them as sellers.

So, your next step in taking control of how you sell and learning how to succeed on your own terms in sales is to stop being salesy. Death to salesy. It doesn't serve your buyers. It doesn't serve you.

Being salesy is the antithesis to everything that is good about sales.

Still, not being salesy almost cost me my job.

When I returned to the office after my two-week sales training indoctrination, I carried an evaluation of my performance written by the course instructor, Jim. It was in a sealed envelope, which I hand-delivered to my big boss, the branch manager, Brian.

Minutes later, Brian summoned me into his office.

"So, how did training go?"

A trap question if I'd ever heard one.

"Uh, yeah, I think it was fine."

"Really? Well, Jim thinks that we should fire you."

I could see the headlines. "Man extinguishes bright future in sales in record time."

Brian went on. "Yes, he thinks that you're—" scanning the page "—too analytical. He says you're not salesy enough. And it's his judgment that you'll never make it as a seller."

Jim thought I should have been fired for not being *salesy*. "Failing" sales training was like a slap to the face to wake me up. If I wanted to be good at sales, I had to figure out how to make sales work for me.

Which I did, through the use of just four factors that enabled me to Sell In with my customers. These are the pillars of Selling In.

1 **Connection:** *Engage* with a buyer on a human level to earn their trust and the permission to stick your nose into their business.

2 **Curiosity:** *Ask great questions* to help the buyer more fully understand the scope and impact of the changes they want to make. And to help them understand what they don't know.

3 **Understanding:** *Listen slowly* to make sure you fully understand what outcomes are most important to the buyer and other parties.

➡ Being salesy is the **antithesis** to everything that is good about sales.

4   **Generosity:** *Enable buyers* by bringing your value and
vision to help them achieve what's most important to
them.

These four surprisingly simple behaviors are the opposite
of salesy. With them you'll build rock-solid, productive,
influence-based relationships that will enable you to succeed on your own terms in the modern sales world. They
will accelerate your ability to help your buyer quickly
gather and make sense of the information they need to
make their choice with the least possible investment of
their time and resources.

These Sell In Pillars are as effective in a virtual or digital sales environment as they are in face-to-face selling.
Human buyers act as humans and receive and process
information as humans, irrespective of the medium of
communication. Though I have flown roughly two million miles in my career, more than 90 percent of my sales
interactions with buyers were done remotely or digitally,
including most of those I describe in this book.

Pro tip: How will you know you're on the right track?
When your buyer tells you, "You don't act like a salesperson." This is one of the greatest compliments that you can
receive. Don't limit yourself to being everyone's stereotype
of a salesperson.

CHAPTER
6

INFLUENCE RULES, PERSUASION DROOLS

F YOU'RE GOING to stop being salesy, then you need to have the right mindset and perspective about the interactions you have with your buyers.

Despite the best efforts of various sales experts and sales trainers to conflate and interchangeably use the words *influence* and *persuasion*, they are not the same thing.

There's a reason Dale Carnegie didn't title his classic book *How to Win Friends and Persuade People*.[4]

To persuade means to prevail on someone to do something by argument, entreaty, or expostulation. To prevail is to gain ascendancy by strength. In other words, to coerce a buyer to do something, which just reinforces their negative image of sellers as sellouts.

If your primary job in sales is to listen to understand what the most important thing is for your buyer, and then help them get that, then what value does persuasion offer? Are you going to persuade the buyer to change their mind about what is most important to them?

Similarly, if your buyer's job is to quickly gather and make sense of the information they need to make a decision to get what is most important to them, then how does persuasion help them achieve that?

Your buyers want you to be a source of value that helps them make informed trade-offs and decisions about how to achieve their most important thing. Which means that your persuasive coercion is of no value to your buyer.

You've been taught and trained that your job is about persuasion; to persuade a buyer that your product must be the solution to their problem. Which is problematic for you. In his book *The Catalyst*, Jonah Berger cites research that shows that people possess a universal resistance to being persuaded. Berger calls it *persuasion reactance*.

We didn't need Berger's fine book to tell us this. We have all personally experienced this resistance, both as sellers and buyers. "No, I'm sure the condo is beautiful. But I'm not in the market for a timeshare."

I believe most sellers are uncomfortable trying to persuade someone who doesn't want to be persuaded. It's human nature. Yet, according to LinkedIn's 2018 State of Sales report, sales bosses spend fifteen billion dollars every year[5] to train sellers to behave in the one way that *every single person in the world instinctively hates*.

Let's face it, persuasion is not a sales skill. It's a blunt instrument of last resort that sellers use when they don't understand how to influence the choices their buyers make. In that sense, influence is the antithesis of persuasion in sales.

Influence is defined as the mental and emotional aptitude to change the actions, understanding, and behavior of other people without the apparent exertion of force. In other words, we use our Connection, Curiosity, Understanding, and Generosity to influence the actions, understanding, and behavior of the buyer.

Sellers who believe that their job is to persuade buyers to purchase their products or services are selling drills. Sellers who help their buyers identify the problems they need to solve and define their options for achieving their desired outcomes are selling holes.

Having an *influence* mindset rather than a *persuasion* mindset alters the nature of how you interact with a buyer. Influence has a positive impact on the experience your buyer has with you. (In contrast to the universal human resistance to being pushed, prodded, and persuaded.)

Here's a simple way to think about the difference between persuasion and influence: If you're a persuasion-based seller, you believe your job is to change the minds of your buyers to buy your product. If you're an influence-based seller, you believe your job is to first understand your buyers and then help them make up their minds about how to solve their problem and achieve their desired outcomes.

➡ Persuasion is a blunt instrument of last resort that sellers use when they don't understand how to **influence the choices** their buyers make.

Persuasion as practiced by most sellers is a zero-sum game. If you're trying to persuade your buyer to change their mind, you are telling them, in essence, "I know better than you. I'm right. And you're wrong." That's Selling Out. Which is not exactly a productive way to strengthen your connection with the buyer.

Contrast that with the buyer's experience with Selling In. The person Selling In doesn't operate on assumptions. Instead, they focus on making the buyer feel heard and understood before recommending a solution.

ARE YOU A SALES LEADER OR MERELY A SALES BOSS?

*Y*OU HAVE A singularly tough job, for which you've received minimal training and support. I get it. I've been there myself. However, just like sellers, you have to make a choice about the type of manager you want to be. You can be a sales leader. Or you can be just a sales boss.

What are the differences between the two? Well, let's start with the basics. Sales leaders know their success flows from helping their people become the best version of themselves. Sales bosses think success is based on driving their people to do more stuff. And then they diverge from there.

Being merely a sales boss isn't helping your sellers. And it certainly isn't helping you achieve the things in your career that are most important to you.

It's time for a change. No one is better positioned to help your sellers stop Selling Out and start Selling In than you.

There will be challenges. For instance, if you're a sales boss, chances are that you work for a sales boss too. So some of this behavior is probably being forced on you.

Again, I get it. But to be the solution, you need the courage to change.

The table on page 62 is a summary of the high-level differences between sales bosses and sales leaders. Which column best describes you?

Though this book is a guide to success for the individual contributor, it also has a lot of lessons for you as a manager who aspires to be a sales leader.

As someone who is responsible for the performance and growth of your sellers, your ambition should never be to make all of your sellers into clones of your "top performer." It won't work. It's counterproductive. Every seller is unique in their mental makeup, mindset, and capabilities, which means that their recipe for personal success is unique to them. You shouldn't try to fit a square peg into the round hole that is your one-size-fits-all sales process.

As a sales leader, you should aspire to help every one of your sellers become the very best version of themselves. This is what they want. This is what you should want. This is the express ticket to faster growth through improved sales performance. And to a team of sellers that are more productive, less stressed, more fulfilled, and prepared to stick around and grow with you.

—

ALSO, AS YOU read this book, you'll hear me tell sellers that they need to push back on orders and suggestions from you that aren't helping them develop and grow. If they want to become the best sales version of themselves, they need to have the autonomy to experiment and fail on their own terms. That may make you nervous because you believe that the certainty of your sales process is what enables individual sales success. Don't kid yourself; it doesn't.

Don't get me wrong. Process is important. But your process works only to the degree that it supports the personal sales process of the individual seller. This book gives sellers the right tools and mindset to develop a successful process of selling that is in alignment with their strengths and with what their buyers need from them to make good decisions. That's how they become the very best version of themselves.

If you support that, it's a win for your buyers, your sellers, and you.

And you'll find yourself evolving from a sales boss into a sales leader.

SALES BOSS LEADER	
SALES BOSS	**SALES LEADER**
Process first	People first
Coaches deals	Coaches people
Trains techniques	Develops capabilities
The science of selling	The art of selling
Enforces compliance	Enables constructive nonconformity
Gives orders	Coaches problem-solving
Applies pressure	Encourages accountability
Risk avoider	Risk taker
Persuasion	Influence
Selling Out	Selling In
Know it all	Learn it all
It's my way or the highway	Whatever's the fastest way I can help you
Inspires anxiety	Inspires change
Top of funnel	Win rate

CHAPTER

7

THERE'S ONE QUESTION EVERY BUYER WILL ASK YOU

VERY EARLY IN my career in sales I made a cold call on the CEO of a large homebuilder in my territory. I was selling computers for what was at the time one of the largest computer companies.

A newly minted sales rep, I was freshly trained in sales and computers. I was twenty-one but looked like I was just shy of my sixteenth birthday. Shoes shined and red power tie straightened, I marched into the lobby and asked the receptionist to see Bill, the CEO.

I fully expected that I was going to be rebuffed so, of course, I was completely taken aback when Bill came into the lobby, shook my hand, and escorted me to his office.

Bill was very polite and completely old-school, even for that era. Silver hair, nice tan, expensive shirt, and slacks that hung just so. He took me into his office, which was empty except for the chairs on either side of his massive wooden desk with a phone on it. He motioned for me to sit down opposite him.

He asked for my business card. I reached over the aircraft carrier–sized surface of the desk and handed it to him. He took it, slowly turned it in his hands, examined it back and front, and laid it on the desk in front of him.

"So, young man, what can I do for you?"

I took a deep breath and launched into my pitch, just as I had been trained to do.

Bill let me talk for about a minute and then raised his hand for me to stop. He opened the top right drawer in his desk and pulled out a rubber band–bound stack of business cards that was literally two inches high.

"These are all the computer salespeople who have been here to see me in the last year." He pulled off the rubber band and spread the cards across the top of his desk like a blackjack dealer in Vegas. There were dozens of cards from every competitor I could think of. As well as from nearly every sales rep from my own branch office. "And I didn't buy a thing from any of them."

He gathered all the business cards back into a neat stack. Except mine.

"So, forget all the other stuff you were just talking about."

He picked up my card, looked at it again, and set it down.

"Mr. Paul, tell me, why should I buy from you?"

The question took me by surprise.

It was clear from the firm tone in his voice and the look in his eyes that the question Bill was asking me wasn't why he should buy a computer from the company I represented.

No. He simply wanted me to answer why he should buy from . . . me.

Why you? he was asking.

And the honest answer to his question was that I had no idea.

Why You?

This is the question that every buyer, every stakeholder in a decision, will ask you. After killing off salesy and putting the lid on persuasion, how you answer this question is the most important step in taking control of how you sell. It's where you irrevocably move from Selling Out to Selling In.

This is such a simple question, but so hard to answer. I don't mean the "Why should I buy from you?" question. Instead, I'm referring to a question we've all been asked hundreds of times in our lives regardless of our profession.

Scan this list and you'll see that hardly a day passes when you aren't asked this question in one form or another.

- Why should I work with you?
- Why should I trust you?
- Why should I invest my time in you?
- Why should I collaborate with you?

- Why should I take advice from you?
- Why should I buy from you?
- Why should I risk my money on you?
- Why should I accept you?
- Why should I hire you?

At heart, these are all the same question.

Scroll through that list of questions again. This time, delete all the words between *Why* and *you*.

You see, the real question that people are asking is "Why...you?"

This is why it's so critically important to be in charge of how you sell. Because you are the difference between winning and losing.

You, the human. Not the company you work for. Not the product you sell.

You.

The answer to this question has very little to do with the brand name of the institution you work for. Or the prestige of the university you attended. Or the past successes on your résumé. Your number of Instagram followers. Who your parents are.

It's not that all of these considerations are unimportant. It's just that they are matters of secondary importance compared to "Why you?"

And you can't be you if you are Selling Out.

➡️ The **"Why you?"** question is not rhetorical. It's an essential question that we all need to be able to answer for anyone we're trying to influence.

The "Why you?" question is not rhetorical. It's an essential question that we all need to be able to answer for anyone we're trying to influence.

In most instances, the question is not asked out loud. However, the buyer is always asking it, whether you hear it or not. And you need to answer it well.

"Why you?" sits at the very heart of some of the most important choices and decisions buyers make. Choices that can affect their careers and lives. Decisions that can affect your career and life.

Why should I trust you to help me identify what is most important to me and to help me get it? Why are you the one to help me solve my problem and reach my desired business outcomes?

There's a reason your buyer accepts your expertise, experience, and insights. They've made a personal judgment about you and your values, your integrity, your credibility, your trustworthiness, and they've made a business judgment about the value that you as an individual can provide to help them achieve what is most important to them.

When you answer the question to the satisfaction of a buyer, an important shift of the buyer-seller dynamic occurs. It changes from a conventional *persuasion*-based "I'm trying to get something from you (i.e., an order)" sales scenario to a dynamic *influence*-based "I have value to give you that will help you make your choices about how to solve your problem" sales scenario.

The words are important. Being salesy is Selling Out. Persuasion is Selling Out. Influence is what your buyers want from you.

In short, "Why you?" simply means one thing: "Why should I (the buyer) provide you (the seller) the opportunity to influence me (and the choices I have to make)?"

Your answer will flow from how you use the four Sell In Pillars to help your buyers achieve what is most important to them.

CHAPTER
8

THE SELL IN PILLARS

SELLING WITHOUT PERSUASION

SPENT A CHUNK of my career selling products that didn't exist.

I know. It sounds like a scam.

I don't mean I was selling typical vaporware or brochureware. Nor was I selling bridges to nowhere.

What I was selling had even less substance than any of those.

I worked for start-up tech companies where my job was to take a bucket of disparate software and hardware technologies and find customers who would pay us millions of dollars to develop and manufacture brand-new products created from those technologies.

There were no brochures. No ideal customer profiles (ICP). No demos. No canned slide decks. No buyer personas.

Let me tell you, this is about the most fun you can have as a seller. Making big deals materialize out of absolutely nothing feels like magic.

The whole process was an interesting puzzle to solve. Since I didn't know what pain points I was addressing or what problem I was solving, defining who my target prospects should be was an exercise in creativity. Furthermore, it was a challenge to determine who at a company was the right person to speak to. And since the people I contacted uniformly had no idea that they had a need for a product that didn't exist, it made the initial sales conversations a bit unpredictable, like driving a car on black ice.

I wasn't selling any one product, yet I was also selling everything: opportunity, choice, freedom, control, vision.

I had to become an expert at selling without persuasion. The old-school persuasion-based sales tactics that had been drilled into me didn't apply for one very simple reason: *You can't persuade someone to buy a solution that doesn't exist to solve a problem they're not aware they have.*

Instead, I had to sell through influence by using the four Sell In Pillars: Connection, Curiosity, Understanding, Generosity.

1 **Connection** enables you to create the human connection through which you build credibility and earn trust with your buyer.

2 **Curiosity** unearths the buyer's challenges, problems, requirements, and future goals. It's about being interested in others before yourself.

3 **Understanding** gives value to the words, goals, and ideas of your buyer. It's not enough to know your buyer's pain points and desired outcomes. You have to understand them and why they are important to your buyer.

4 **Generosity** is about giving things that are of value to the buyer in order to help them achieve what is most important to them.

These pillars formed the structure of how I interacted with my buyers.

I made a **Connection** with executives at all levels within my targeted accounts by asking Insight Questions to trigger conversations (see Chapter 10 for examples). I kept abreast of all the current trends and business developments happening in my industry, so as I built personal connections throughout these companies, I became a credible and trusted source of information and insight for a wide range of stakeholders. (And I answered their "Why you?" question in the process.)

I focused my **Curiosity** on asking questions that would identify key market opportunities the buyer was interested in capturing but lacked the internal know-how and capabilities to address. I used great follow-up questions to explore in-depth with each major stakeholder what the most important thing was to them and where the gaps were that prevented them from achieving it.

I used my deep **Understanding** of the buyer to engage them in a collaborative process to help them understand their market vulnerabilities and potential upsides. And to help make sure we understood their internal constraints. Through this work, we'd converge on a mutual understanding of what a compelling business opportunity was for them and how we could help them capitalize on it.

Since I wasn't selling a product, I focused my **Generosity** on providing value that would help create a detailed vision of what success would look like to the buyer if we worked together. In the process, I co-created value with the stakeholders that helped them identify opportunities for transformation that they hadn't yet recognized. I provided information and insights that helped them understand trade-offs that would enable them to plan and execute a program that hadn't previously been on their strategic roadmap.

In short, I used the four Sell In Pillars to help my buyers create a vision in their own minds of what success would look like for them if they invested in developing and selling a product that didn't yet exist to capitalize on an opportunity in a market they didn't yet serve.

This is the perspective and mindset you need to have every time you engage with a new buyer. Your buyers can get product features, technical specifications, and pricing from the internet. What they can't get from your website are the questions, context, insights, and other forms of value that help them fully understand their problem and visualize what success looks like. That comes from how you are Selling In: the Connection, Curiosity, Understanding, and Generosity they can only get from you, the human seller.

Using the Pillars to Answer "Why You?"

A substantial portion of every purchase decision is based on how the buyer feels about their experience working with you, the seller.

When you interact with buyers using the four Sell In Pillars (Connection, Curiosity, Understanding, Generosity), you will have an impact on the people asking, "Why you?" Why should they invest their time and attention in you? Why should they trust you? Why should they allow you the opportunity to influence the choices and decisions they have to make?

That's why Selling Out is so problematic. Being on the receiving end of salesy is not a good experience for the buyer. And while that might not completely slam the door on your chances of winning your buyer's business, it certainly doesn't help you.

When you use the Sell In Pillars, your buyers will feel:

Connected: When you connect with someone at a human level you make them feel a part of something bigger than themselves. They have become a part of your network. As you build a relationship with that person, you represent new possibilities to them—possibilities for connection, and for growth. In addition, being connected is the pathway to trust. Being open and vulnerable is not just a way to build trust with someone. It also makes the other person feel trusted. That opens the door to influence.

Interesting: It's really very simple. When you are curious and demonstrate a sincere interest about another person, you make them feel interesting. That builds their sense of self-worth. Everyone believes they have something to offer to others, if only someone cared to ask. (That someone will be you.)

Understood: When you ask questions to truly understand what's most important to another person, you come to understand not only how they feel, but also *why* they feel the way they do. Understanding this context is the key to making people feel understood, and it is the very definition of empathy. Being more empathetic enables you to make better decisions about how to help someone achieve their goals.

Valued: When you make a person feel understood, you make them feel valued. When you're generous and give something of value to someone, you make them feel valued. You trigger potential reciprocity. If you're a salesperson and you share an insight with a prospect that helps them better understand the problem they're trying to solve, that new knowledge will make the prospect feel valued. In addition, with this new knowledge, the person potentially can increase their contribution to the greater good of their own organization. In this way, they then become more valued within their organization.

Let's go through each Sell In Pillar in turn.

CHAPTER
9

CONNECTION

AYA ANGELOU, THE great American poet, famously said, "People will forget what you said. People will forget what you did. People will never forget how you made them feel." Connecting is about how *human* you make other people feel. It's how they experience you. It is not a judgment about your worth as a human being.

Connecting on a human level is more about who you are than what you know or what you do. It's about how a buyer experiences you—your values and character.

Look at your own experience buying products or services. Or your experience paying for advice. It doesn't matter whether it's for personal or business purposes. Think back to all the salespeople, real estate agents, doctors, financial advisors, therapists, and others that you have chosen to work with in your life.

Before making that choice, how often did you say to yourself, "You know, I'm not sure I really trust this financial advisor. But what the heck, I'm going to invest my money

➡ You can't pitch someone on why they should trust you. You can't explain to someone why they should build a relationship with you. **They have to experience you.**

with her anyway." Or "This painting contractor kind of gives me the creeps. But I'm going to use him anyway."

The answer is never. You didn't. And your buyers ask the same exact question about you. Don't believe anyone who tells you differently. Good things rarely happen in sales without that human-to-human connection. It's possible. But not highly probable.

Think about influence from your buyers' perspective. When they decide that they have to interact with one or more salespeople, they have a choice. They have a limited amount of time to devote to this task. Therefore, they have to carefully choose which sellers are worth the investment of their time and attention. Which one(s) will help increase their chances of achieving their desired outcomes? Whom should they allow to influence the choices they have to make?

You can't pitch someone on why they should trust you. You can't explain to someone why they should build a relationship with you. They have to experience you.

In *The Challenger Sale*, Brent Adamson and Matthew Dixon wrote that 53 percent of the buyer decision is based on their buying experience. That's their experience of you. So, when you make the decision to take control of who you are as a seller, to sell without selling out, you will be influencing how the buyer experiences you. You will be answering the question, "Why you?"

Connection is the Building Block of Influence

I'm going to repeat that because I don't want you to miss it.

Connection is the building block of influence.

And it's cemented into place by the three other Sell In Pillars: Curiosity, Understanding, and Generosity.

Connection in sales serves two purposes. First, you want your buyers to view you as a person who can help them achieve the thing that's most important to them—a desired business outcome. Second, to do that requires that you and the buyer stop being strangers. It requires that you create a positive perception in the mind of the buyer. You want them to think of you as a person and a resource that can deliver value to them. It requires that buyers feel the interest, respect, and empathy you have for them. It requires that the buyers perceive, and believe, that you have the credibility and trustworthiness to help them make important trade-offs and decisions.

Connection is the gateway to learning and understanding what is important to another person and how you can make it happen for them. Connection is the portal through which the buyer experiences you and through which you develop the necessary empathy, credibility, and trust that enable you to help your buyer.

It's why Connection is so central to establishing your influence.

Your buyers want to do business with people with whom they feel a level of connection and trust. Your ability to influence starts with the moment of connection.

Your motivation for building a strong human connection with your buyer should simply be, "How can I help you achieve what's important for you?"

Connection is the opposite of what we all experience on LinkedIn and other online platforms. There, it's about one thing: "I want to connect with you so I can pitch you something." Social media is the home of the "What can you do for me?" ethos.

In his book *Never Eat Alone*, Keith Ferrazzi uses the phrase, "What's the fastest way I can help you?" I love that. It's not about reciprocity, as in you scratch my back and I'll scratch yours. Instead it's a clear acknowledgment that in today's sales environment, the surest path to achieving one's own goals is to ensure that other people achieve theirs. "I listen to the buyer to define and understand what's the most important thing to them. Then I help them get it."

That journey starts with a human connection with your buyer.

Let's review how to make that happen.

Be a Good Human

What's the not-so-secret secret to connecting with a buyer?

It's simple: be a good human.

Be respectful. Be curious and interested in the other person. Be other-oriented. Be helpful. Add value.

You'd think that I shouldn't have to state the obvious. Unfortunately, I do. There are some who'd have you believe that a good connection with a buyer isn't that vital. They are wrong. Feel free to take your chances with that approach. It won't work.

It costs you absolutely nothing to be a good person. It doesn't take more time. It doesn't take any money. It's one of the few things in sales that is truly easy to do and that is completely under your control.

Here are some surefire ways to connect with your buyers, in person or remotely.

First Impressions are Forever

Making a positive first impression on a buyer does not happen by chance. It is not one of those "they either like me or they don't" moments. You have control over the impression you create.

When two people first meet, each forms their impression of the other person in as little as 250 milliseconds. That's the time it takes to blink.

Here's the rub. Research has found that these first impressions are sticky, meaning they aren't easily changed. Even when people are presented evidence that contradicts their initial opinion of another person, they rarely change their minds.

What does this mean for you? That it's absolutely essential for you to make a positive, and memorable, first impression on your potential buyers.

My parents drilled the power of the first impression into me: "You get only one chance to make a good first impression," they repeated. At times, I felt that my parents were so insistent that my siblings and I learn good manners because they were afraid of us embarrassing them in a social setting. While there was some truth in that, in retrospect, I think that they were equally focused on making certain that we didn't embarrass ourselves.

Be respectful.

Be friendly.

Don't assume anything. (For instance, don't assume that it's okay to call the fifty-year-old CEO of your buyer "pal.")

Big Returns on Small Talk

There will be sales bosses who tell you not to use small talk with buyers. They will try to persuade you that buyers don't like it or don't have time for it. And I am telling you that those who give you this bad advice are dead wrong. Don't take that advice. (In my experience, those who argue most strenuously against small talk are generally not good at it. So take their advice with a large grain of salt.)

The science is clear that small talk is essential to connecting and building relationships.[6]

In fact, small talk makes you happy. That being said, don't overdo it. A few minutes to start a call or meeting is okay. Beyond that, you're digging into time reserved for business.

Here's my favorite small-talk starter. It's contrary to the advice that any sales boss or sales trainer will give. I ask about the weather. You see, everyone experiences weather. If you want to quickly establish common ground with a buyer, ask about the one experience you know you have in common.

But be advised: There's a good way to ask about the weather. And a bad way.

The *bad* way to ask—"Hey, how's the weather out there?"—is lazy and pointless. Instead, prior to your call, check the weather where the buyer is located. "I see you're getting hammered with a blizzard today. Snow day for the kids? I loved those as a kid. What was your favorite movie to watch on a snow day?" Use the shared general experience of weather to bridge into a shared personal experience that creates a connection.

That's what *I* have found to be effective. There are a ton of other small-talk openers. Google "small talk conversation starters" if you need ideas. And use LinkedIn and other social media as great sources of information about the interests of your buyer that you could use to establish common ground.

Invest in a bit of small talk. It works.

Don't Shift Your Support

Along the same lines, one of the easiest ways to stop a connection dead in its tracks is to turn a conversation and make it all about you. Sellers do this all the time without realizing it. They believe that they are establishing common ground with a buyer when they are really just throwing cold water on the connection.

We've all been guilty of this. I know I have.

Imagine you're in a conversation with a buyer. The buyer shares a story about anything; it could be about business, or it could be personal. Let's say that on a recent family vacation everything went awry when they got to their destination hotel and the hotel claimed to have no record of his reservation.

You have a choice in how to respond. You could say, "That had to have been horrible. I know just how you felt—something similar happened to me on vacation last summer. We got to the hotel and..." Or you could say, "That had to have been horrible. How did you feel when the clerk said you had no reservation? Were you able to get your rooms? How did your vacation turn out?"

The first response is called a *shift response*. You might believe that you're establishing common ground with the buyer by talking about how you shared the same experience. However, what's really happening is that you shifted the focus of the conversation from the buyer to you. It's like you told the buyer, "That's an interesting story. But mine is even more interesting."

The second response is what's known as a *support response*. You're showing real concern, empathy, and support for the buyer. You're keeping the focus of the conversation on the buyer and not drawing attention to yourself.

Which one do you think is more effective in building a connection with another person?

Be Interested. Be Interesting.

The simplest way for you to make yourself interesting to another person is to be interested in that person. As humans, we are drawn to those who show an interest in us.

Put yourself in the position of a buyer who receives calls from two sellers. One makes a pitch for his product. The other seller asks relevant questions about you, your history, and your requirements. Which one would you reward with your attention?

Let's take that one step further. Do you know how to make a friend?

I hesitate to use the word *friend* in this context because you are not trying to become friends with your buyers. Friendly, yes. Friends, no. However, I bring it up because research has found that the key to successfully connecting with someone you've just met is knowing how to make a friend. Yep. That's it. Make a friend.

So, visualize yourself in a social setting. You were just introduced to someone at a party. A friend of a friend. What do you say to them? Do you immediately ask them to give you something? Of course not.

When you meet someone new in a purely social setting, you don't think only of what that person can do for you. You show a genuine interest in that person and try to establish a bond based on a common interest. And that's all you need to do when you're connecting with a buyer.

The next time you speak with a potential buyer for the first time, imagine instead that you're meeting them at a party, at your kid's school, or in some non-business setting. In that environment, ask yourself, what's the first question I'd normally ask a new acquaintance?

Connecting is simple. Be more interested in others than in yourself.

WAIT: Why Am I Talking?

Just a quick reminder that when you're trying to build a connection with another human, your objective is to learn about them. Which means you have to let them do the talking.

Tom Hanks is one of my favorite actors. I read an interview with him in which he spoke about what he does when he finds himself in a meeting where it's important for him to understand the needs and perspectives of the other party.[7] He uses the acronym WAIT as a reminder to himself about the importance of asking great questions and listening.

WAIT = Why Am I Talking?

It's so simple. If you're on a sales call, tell yourself to WAIT. Why am I talking if I'm trying to connect with this person? Why am I talking if I need to learn about this person and their needs? Why am I talking if I need to develop an in-depth understanding of what the most important thing is to this buyer?

Then shut up and listen.

The Ask 5 Rule

Imagine you're in an interview for a job. Instead of waiting for the interviewer to kick things off, you ask a question first: "I know you probably have a list of questions to ask me, but would you mind if I start by asking you a question?"

Bang! That's a badass Connection move. Now you're in control of the narrative.

Remember, you become interesting to other people by being interested in what's important to them (and, ultimately, you).

Here's an easy technique you can use to kick-start a productive conversation with a buyer. I call it the Ask 5 Rule. It means that you have to ask a minimum of five questions of the buyer before they ask their first question of you. This is especially effective for a first sales conversation, and it takes just a bit of preparation.

Ideally your first five questions should be layered, meaning that each question builds on the one you just asked. Here's an example:

1 Where are you from originally?
2 What sort of work did you do there?
3 Did your work bring you here?
4 How was that transition for you?
5 What are the big differences you've found living here?

If you want to practice your Ask 5 before you spring it on a buyer, try it in a social setting. It could be a back-to-school night. A party. A networking event. A wedding. When you're standing next to a stranger in the buffet line, ask them your first question. Then see if you can ask four more questions before you have to answer a question about yourself. It's not awkward, honestly. Practice every opportunity you have. It helps.

And, no, "Hi, I'm Andy. What's your name?" doesn't count as one of your Ask 5.

All Empathy Is Not Equal

You have to use the right empathy in creating a connection with your buyers.

The *right empathy*?

Not all empathy is equal. Nor does it all have the same value for buyers.

There can be no disagreement that empathy is an essential and critical part of forming a connection with another human. However, empathy comes in several forms. And the particular form of empathy that is the most useful to you as a seller develops from listening and understanding: *cognitive empathy* is you having a clear idea *why* they feel the way they do.

The default empathy sellers are trained to feel is the classic "put yourself in your buyer's shoes" empathy.

That's *compassionate empathy*. The "I understand how they feel" type.

The problem with compassionate empathy is that feeling is not enough. The empathy you can effectively use to help your buyer is not about simply knowing how someone feels. It's about understanding *why* they feel the way they do.

Understanding how a buyer feels doesn't give you any useful information that enables you to help them. You know their current state, but you don't understand how they got into that state or what to do next.

On the other hand, if you understand *why* the buyer feels the way they do, then you begin to understand their situation and perspective. You begin to understand the context of their challenges, and what's most important to them, which helps crystalize the opportunities you have to help them.

Unfortunately, our tendency to dramatize the world around us extends to our perception of our buyer's situation. In short, your feelings get in the way of developing a true understanding, and the necessary empathy, for a buyer.

I see too many sellers assume, having read a persona description of their buyer, that they are now empathetic to their situation. They're not. You're not. Empathy requires a dialogue with your buyer. It requires asking a variety of questions. Most importantly, it requires that you listen slowly and carefully to their answers. (More on this in Chapter 11: Understanding.)

Feeling without understanding is sympathy. It may seem like a small difference, but buyers don't want your sympathy. They want your understanding. And they can tell the difference.

So, what are you missing without empathy? You're missing the opportunity to connect on a human level with your buyers. You're missing the opportunity for true Understanding, a core Sell In Pillar.

Assume that you've done a good job of using the factors of the Sell In Pillars to build rapport with the buyer, asking great questions and better follow-up questions to learn the information you need to develop a good understanding of the buyer's needs and how you can best be of service to them.

What's often missing is the context for that information—that is, understanding the *why*. For instance, Why is this important to the buyer? Why is it important for the buyer to solve this problem? What are the consequences for the organization if the problem doesn't get solved? What are the potential consequences for the buyer if the problem is left unsolved?

Listening carefully and asking great follow-up questions uncovers where that gold is buried. In other words, listening to understand can put you on the winning path because you're persisting and digging, and you're truly understanding.

Trust the MICE

To earn someone's trust, and ultimately the permission to influence them, you must first be worthy of that trust. How do you decide if someone is trustworthy? What does your buyer require from you to earn their trust?

We talk about the importance of credibility and trust all the time in sales and business. Most of us acknowledge that trust, or the lack of trust, is an issue. And that building trust is the central challenge in forming effective relationships with buyers. However, we usually believe that the absence of trust is someone else's fault, which is a problem.

Stephen R. Covey writes, "As long as you think the problem is out there, that very thought is the problem."

Building trust starts with you.

There are four essential elements that must be present to build trust with a buyer. I've created a simple acronym to help you remember them: MICE.

Motives: Are your motives transparent to the buyer?

Integrity: Do your actions align with your words?

Credibility: Do you have the knowledge and capabilities to perform?

Execution: Are you living up to the commitments you've made?

Let's dive into these in detail.

Motives: Be Transparent in Your Motivations

"The moment there is suspicion about a person's motives, everything he does becomes tainted." So said Mahatma Gandhi. Suspicion is death to trustworthiness and influence. Obviously, you want to avoid that.

Motives mean that you're working with your buyers from the perspective of service and with the objective of helping them achieve the thing that is most important to them. Your agenda must be transparent so that they feel that your actions are totally in support of their needs and requirements.

In the context of building a connection with another person, you should be completely transparent about your motives in dealing with them.

Unlike a magician who says "See? Nothing in my hands, and nothing up my sleeves," you have a responsibility to make sure that your motives are transparent to everyone concerned.

Think about it this way. Imagine that before meeting a buyer for the first time, you take a Sharpie and inscribe your motivation for working with the buyer in indelible black ink on your forehead so that it is clear for everyone to see and understand. What would you write? Probably something like "Help you achieve your desired business outcomes." (Write small!)

How would publicly advertising your motives like this change how you act?

We've all experienced the inherent distrust of salespeople in our buyers. Buyers typically don't give us the benefit of the doubt. They assume that we're all first and foremost self-interested. "What's in it for me?" So, turn that assumption on its ear. Whatever you want to achieve with a buyer, make your motivations visible to everyone.

For every sales opportunity you're pursuing, you have to bear in mind that the buyer is asking themselves, "Is this seller worthy of our trust?" So, you must be able to answer the following questions for each deal you're working:

- What are my motives in helping this buyer? (Besides just getting an order.)
- Why do I actually want their business?
- What's in it for them (that they can only get from me)?
- Have I shared my motives with the buyer?

Transparency gives you the opportunity, if not the responsibility, to demolish the negative stereotype of salespeople with every buyer you work with.

Integrity: Align Your Actions with Your Words

Integrity means that there is alignment between your words and your actions. This congruence of thoughts, words, and actions is what buyers quickly perceive when they decide whether or not to invest some of their time and attention in building a trusted relationship with you.

You can't pursue an agenda that puts your interests before theirs while hiding behind the facade of telling someone you want to help them. Well, you can. However, there's a term for that: *narcissist*. For now, let's just call it untrustworthy. Acting in this way could be damaging to them or their careers. To be trustworthy, you have to ensure that every action you take with a buyer aligns with the motivations you shared with them.

One of my favorite quotations about trust is widely attributed to Ralph Waldo Emerson: "What you do speaks so loudly, I cannot hear what you say." In short, your actions speak louder than your words. If you don't operate with integrity, then your actions will betray your words. And the buyer will believe that you're not trustworthy.

What follows is an example of a scenario I frequently see played out with sales teams, one that irrevocably damages current and future sales opportunities with buyers. Has this happened to you? I had it happen to me when I was a relatively new individual contributor.

I had developed an exciting prospect for a big sales opportunity. Several of my biggest competitors were chasing the deal as well. But I had forged a strong connection with the customer, demonstrated my trustworthiness, and given us a competitive edge in the process. Our deal was

→ Your actions speak louder than your words.

scheduled to be approved by the buyer's board of directors in late July. However, my boss's boss, the almighty regional VP, decided that this opportunity had to close in June in order for him to hit his quarterly number.

At that point, my motivations didn't matter. I was ordered to accelerate the close of my deal by thirty days. I dutifully met with my buyer and explained the situation. In that moment, in the eyes of my buyer, I morphed from a trusted advisor into a slick-talking "what's it going to take to get you into this car today" hustler. He was unmoved. He said that they still had work to do before they could present their case to the board. My boss was on the phone with me every five minutes telling me to offer an escalating scale of discounts to close the deal. I was up to nearly a 50 percent discount when the customer kicked me out of his office.

Everything I had told the buyer about being there to help them was shown to be false. All trust was lost.

I see this pattern played out every month by sales bosses. "Screw what you told the buyer. Just go get the deal." You can. But any trust you've built will disappear. The buyer will know that you're truly interested in only one thing. You may get the deal because they can't pass up the discount. But they'll churn and move to a new vendor as soon as they can.

Credibility: Demonstrate Competence

Credibility means that you demonstrate that you possess the capabilities, knowledge, and skills to help your buyers achieve their desired results; to get the thing that is most important to them.

In other words, your buyer perceives that you have the credibility to help them solve their problem and achieve their desired business outcomes.

To build your credibility, it's equally important to be open with your buyer about what you know and what you don't know. Anytime you are building an influence connection, the buyer wants to be comfortable that you know what you're talking about. That you possess some level of expertise and experience in your field. After all, they are opening themselves up to your influence. But you don't have to be the absolute expert to build credibility. You don't want to pretend to possess knowledge, experience, or expertise that you don't have.

There are two buckets of credibility. One is knowledge-based credibility. It contains your product knowledge and your understanding of how your products are used, your understanding of your customer and their business, as well as your industry knowledge, experience, and expertise. The second is your personal credibility. Are you open and transparent about what you know and what you don't yet understand? Are you open about your motivations? Do you appear trustworthy by not misrepresenting what you know?

You'll build more credibility by admitting to what you don't know, rather than attempting to bluff your way through answering a question that tests your knowledge.

There is always a push-pull when you want to demonstrate the value you can bring to a situation. You might ask yourself, "What's the harm in stretching the truth just a little to show myself in the best light?" Potentially everything.

There is a quote commonly attributed to Mark Twain: "If you tell the truth, you don't have to remember anything." In other words, if you don't make yourself out to be more than you are, you never have to worry about being exposed for being less than that.

Execution: Meet Your Commitments

People often talk about sales as being a series of commitments that you extract from the buyer. However, as a seller you make a large number of your own commitments throughout your sales process.

Execution, as a trust builder, means that you live up to all the commitments you make to help your buyers achieve their goals. If you commit to responding to a question by a certain date and time, you must respond by that date and time. If you schedule a customer call for a particular hour, be there five minutes early. If you schedule a demo with a buyer, do the appropriate discovery and preparation to ensure the demo is a productive and effective use of the buyer's time and attention.

I could go on with examples, but you get the point.

Be proactive about making commitments and giving yourself deadlines regarding your sales activities during the buyer's journey. And then live up to them. Because the buyer is keeping score.

This is not only a differentiator and trust builder. It's also giving the buyer a taste of what it will be like to work with your company after the deal is closed and implementation begins.

Take a Risk on Yourself

The last word about trust.

Risk is essential to building trust.

Risk? I'll bet you were expecting me to say vulnerability.

They go hand in hand. You have to take a risk to be vulnerable. Just be careful not to overdo it.

The old-school way of looking at vulnerability and trust was that trust enabled you to be vulnerable with another person. In other words, trust was a requirement for vulnerability. More recently, science has shown that it actually works the other way around.[8] Taking the risk to be vulnerable with another person actually leads to trust building. The willingness to be vulnerable demonstrates trustworthiness.

But what type of vulnerability do you need to display?

Sales trainers often talk of vulnerability in the sense of classic emotional vulnerability. "I'm going to share a personal story with a buyer that illustrates something important about me." Sometimes that can work. Sometimes there's common ground that can be found with a buyer over personal vulnerability. However, in this social media age, there's always a risk of oversharing and revealing something personal of yourself that makes the buyer uncomfortable. That's not what you're going for.

Instead, think of personal vulnerability in a business context. My friend Charlie Green is one of the leading authorities on trust in business. He is the co-author of *The Trusted Advisor* and author of *Trust-Based Selling*. He has a technique he recommends sellers use to demonstrate vulnerability in a way that is relevant to the buyer's situation. He calls it BARG, which stands for Bring a Risky Gift.

What this means is you, the seller, take the risk to share something with your buyer that you believe would help them in their buying journey, but that they may not readily welcome or accept. This could be a new idea about how to think about the outcomes they're trying to achieve. It could be data about how their company's performance compares to others that you work with. It could be a suggestion about how to implement your solution.

Regardless of whether the buyer accepts the gift, BARG demonstrates a willingness on your part to take the risk, to be vulnerable, to inject some uncertainty in the buying process and your own chances of winning the deal, in order to help the buyer make a better choice. This selfless alignment with the best interests of the buyer is a key contributor to building trust.

Everything Is Connected

Before we move on, let's connect the dots.

A strong trust-based Connection with a buyer makes them more receptive to your Curiosity.

In the absence of trust, a buyer will be less likely to fully answer the questions you ask. That's a normal human reaction. And if the buyer holds back information from you, then that hampers your ability to reach a full Understanding of the things that are most important to them.

And this lack of Understanding deflates the value of your Generosity because the value you give the buyer may completely miss the mark of what they need from you to make a good decision.

Everything is connected.

CHAPTER 10

CURIOSITY

THE LATE ANTHONY Bourdain used his food travelogue series to connect with people from all cultures in every corner of the world in order to learn about them and their stories. Bourdain said: "What I do is not complicated. Any stranger who shows an honest curiosity about what the locals think is the best food is going to be welcomed. When you eat their food, and you seem happy, people sitting around a table open up and interesting things happen."

Think about this in the context of what we do as sellers.

If you meet a new prospect and default to the rote, uninterested interrogation of them with your list of scripted questions, then that door will be closed to you.

If you meet a new prospect and show an honest curiosity in them, and the things that are important to them, then you will be welcomed. And when your buyers respond to your curiosity, opening up and talking about the things that are most important to them, that's when interesting things happen.

Use your curiosity to find the story in every one of your buyers. Learn what is the most important thing to them, and how you can help them get it.

All I Had Were Questions

I don't possess the sales gene.

I know. I'm hopeless.

I have taken multiple sales "personality tests" (or is it sales multiple personality tests?) that claim to unerringly uncover a person's suitability for a career in sales. I've failed these in the worst ways possible. I took one of the major sales assessment tests a couple of years ago, and my score was so shockingly low, the CEO of the company called me to see if I was feeling okay. I think he was concerned that I'd had a breakdown. I assured him I was fine.

Even though I've personally sold hundreds of millions of dollars in complex systems to enterprises around the world and helped client companies sell hundreds of millions more, according to these tests, I don't possess any sales DNA. Nope. I don't have whatever it takes to succeed in sales.

When I graduated from college, I had no discernible job skills. What I did have, and still have, was an insatiable curiosity (and a competitive streak a mile wide). Naturally, I went into sales.

Asking questions is how I engage with the world and understand new concepts. Asking questions is how I've developed the acumen that has enabled me to ask even better, more insightful questions.

Through your questions, you build a connection with your buyer. It's through your questions that you learn what's most important to your buyers and understand how you can help them get it. And it's through your questions that you understand the value you need to give your buyers to help them make their choices.

After all, as Clayton Christensen wrote, "Questions are places in your mind where answers fit. If you haven't asked the question, the answer has nowhere to go." [9]

Questions Make Room for Answers in Your Mind

To make room in your mind for answers, you have to ask good questions. Good questions are those you don't know the answer to ahead of time. Consuming the time of your buyer to ask the same list of questions you ask every other buyer isn't a display of Curiosity; it's lazy indifference.

This has probably happened to you: at some point in your onboarding or training you were handed a list of questions to ask your buyer and were told their answers "should sort of look something like [this]" based on their persona. Which means that you'll get just enough information to "sort of" understand what the buyer is trying to achieve.

As I've said, sales success comes from listening to understand what the most important thing is to your buyer and helping them get it. The unspoken part of that equation is that before you listen, you have to be curious and ask great questions that uncover the information that will enable you to truly understand what's most important. You have to deploy Curiosity to dig wider and deeper to make that happen.

Of course, this can't happen if you haven't first built a solid connection. Buyers don't volunteer information about the things that are most important to them just because you ask them. How often do you share personal information with strangers? A person has to earn the right to receive that information by establishing some level of personal connection, credibility, and trust. Right?

Four Keys to Unlock Your Curiosity

Curiosity is as important as intelligence: Research suggests that your curiosity (CQ) is just as reliable a predictor of success as your intelligence (IQ) and emotional intelligence (EQ). Why? Curious people deploy their curiosity to better navigate the ambiguity of complex problem-solving environments—which describes basically every sales opportunity you will work on.

Curiosity is a conversation trigger for your buyers: When you pose a great question to your buyer, you force them to think, which invariably leads them to ask you a question. The buyer just made room for your answer by asking their question. This pattern creates a virtuous circle of question and answer that we normally call a conversation.

Curiosity requires intellectual humility: Intellectual humility means having an open mind and the willingness to admit what you don't know. Salespeople generally hate to admit what they don't know. That shows as a lack of integrity. Think about it this way: A person Selling Out is a know-it-all. A person Selling In is a learn-it all. If you want to make an impression with a buyer, you can do so much more effectively through the questions you ask than by trying to be persuasive with features and benefits. One requires understanding. The other is just annoying.

Curiosity requires persistence: The curious seller is never satisfied that they have all the information they need. Think about this quote from Jonas Salk, the discoverer of the polio vaccine: "What people think of as the moment of discovery is really the discovery of the question." The moment you think you know everything is the moment you need to crank up your curiosity.

➡ **Curious people** deploy their curiosity to better navigate the ambiguity of complex problem-solving environments.

Why Do You Ask?

Why do we ask questions?

There are two goals of asking great questions. The first is for you to understand the buyer. And, once you understand, to make your buyer feel understood. The second goal is to trigger questions and thoughts in the mind of your buyer about what they are trying to accomplish. You're attempting to help the buyer develop a better understanding of the nature and scope of the problem they are trying to solve.

Imagine you have an important call with a buyer scheduled for today. During this call you can take only one of two actions to help your buyer move closer to making a purchase decision: You can share a business insight or story with the buyer. Or you can ask them a question.

Which action would you take? I'd go with the question every time. Because the answer I receive will enable me to learn and understand something more about the buyer.

You'll know you're on the right track when the buyer tells you, "Wow, a seller has never asked me that question before."

Think of the many ways questions are useful to your buyer and you. Questions

- deepen your connection with your buyer;
- activate the interest of your buyer;
- reveal new insights to your buyer;

- challenge your buyer to think, or rethink;
- deepen your understanding of the buyer and their requirements;
- reveal decision criteria; and
- reveal barriers to change and success.

The point is that your list of scripted discovery questions reveals just the tip of the iceberg. You have to go deeper to really understand what's most important to your buyer and how you can help them get it.

As one famous French maxim goes, "Judge a man by his questions rather than his answers." That's how you want your buyers to assess your value.

The Two Answers Every Seller Needs

In general, you're trying to learn everything you can that will enable you to help your buyer make a good decision with the least investment of time and resources.

In particular, you're trying to learn and understand two things:

1 **What is the one thing that is the most important to the buyer?** There's always one thing. You need to find it. In every deal I won, from a ten-thousand-dollar deal to a fifty-million-dollar deal, there was always one thing, one problem, or one outcome that was more important to the critical decision maker than anything else.

2   To whom specifically is this one thing most important?
   Even in the era of increasing consensus-driven decision-making, not every individual's opinion carries the
   same weight. Despite appearances, some stakeholders are more equal than others. Find out what is most
   important to those folks, and you'll be on the inside
   track.

The Right Time to Ask Questions

What is the right time to ask questions? All the time. Just
when you think you've learned everything there is to know
about your buyer, ask more questions.

Most sellers are trained to consider the "discovery
stage" of their sales process as the time and place for them
to ask the bulk of their questions. Don't fall into the trap
that says discovery takes place in a single stage of the buyer's journey.

You should ask questions in every single interaction you
have with a buyer. It doesn't matter whether it's a sales call,
phone call, demo, text, email, or social touch.

The basis of influence is understanding. That means
that you can never stop learning and deepening your
understanding about the requirements of the buyer, about
what's most important to them, and about their desired
business outcomes. You'll learn the answer to that question only by continuing to ask questions.

Ask. Don't Tell.

The temptation to talk about yourself is the antithesis of Curiosity. Unfortunately, that temptation runs strong in all of us, especially when we're in a situation where we want to explain ourselves. Or justify ourselves. Or to show off just how much we think we know about a particular topic.

Here's a simple way to convert the impulse to talk about yourself into a great question habit. Anytime you feel the need to say something about yourself (including talking about your product) phrase it as a question instead.

For example, imagine that you're a salesperson, and you feel the burning need to tell a potential buyer about your latest product feature. You have a choice. You could tell the buyer, "Hey, I don't know if you saw this, but we just announced this cool new feature that enables you to fully automate your XYZ process." Alternatively, you could ask, "If you could fully automate your XYZ process, what impact would that have on your sales growth?"

When your convert your statement of fact into an Impact Question (see page 127), it makes a statement about you to the buyer that you possess some acumen that enables you to see the bigger picture.

Every chance you have: Ask. Don't tell.

A Mini-Guide to Questions

I use six different types of questions. All are useful, and sometimes quite necessary, for sellers and their buyers:

1 Who, What, When Questions
2 Impact Questions
3 Trade-off Questions
4 Vision Questions
5 Insight Questions
6 Follow-up Questions

Who, What, When Questions

Who, What, When Questions are very much the same basic questions that all journalists are trained to ask in order to get a full picture of the situation on which they're reporting (sometimes called W5). These are your classic discovery questions: Who? What? When? Where? Why? How?

You've heard these a million times in class. Or in movies and TV shows. The cub reporter is being drilled by her world-weary editor about the necessity to report on the facts. What are the facts?

Part of selling is like being a reporter. You need to gather the facts of the buyer before you can dig deeper into their story. You have to write the news article before you can write the in-depth feature article that provides context to the facts.

In other words, you need to understand the facts of the buyer's situation (problems, pain points, challenges, roadblocks) before you get into the larger picture of their motivations, goals, ambitions, and outcomes.

- Who (is involved in decision-making, responsible for this purchase)?

- What (is the pain point, roadblock, obstacle you're facing)?

- When (did this problem start and how long has it been a problem)?

- Where (in your organization is this pain being felt)?

- How (did this problem occur and has anything changed)?

- Why (did you decide to address this problem now)?

Note that none of these Who, What, When Questions are the dreaded closed-ended scripted questions that get only yes or no answers. Those questions help neither the buyer nor the seller. These are great questions because they all have the possibility of opening the door to a great follow-up question.

You can also layer these questions together for a more complex discovery scenario, like a basic gap analysis with a buyer. In a gap analysis, a seller asks questions that prompt the buyer to compare their current state with their desired future state. This shines a light on the gap between where the buyer is now and where they want to be at some point in the future. Helping the buyer to bridge that gap represents your potential sales opportunity.

That would look something like this:

1 What are the outcomes you envision achieving with this purchase?

2 What's the timeframe you have to achieve that?

3 Where do you stand today in relation to achieving that defined outcome?

4 What are the internal and external roadblocks that are currently preventing you from achieving those desired short-term and longer term outcomes?

5 What are the risks to the organization in terms of standing still and deciding to maintain the status quo?

6 What is the value, in dollars, of achieving your desired outcomes in those timeframes?

Impact Questions

Buying and selling are all about making a change. Any change will have an impact on the person or people involved with making the choices and decisions associated with a purchase on both a company and personal level.

Impact Questions are those that surface the specific ways that making the change will impact the buying organization, from the top all the way down to the individual.

If your objective is Selling In, then Impact Questions provide the context you need to ask more questions, tell more stories, and relate your value proposition in a way that is personalized to the buyer.

Think about Impact Questions as layers in a stack. Always start with the impact for the largest entity (Layer 1), then work your way down to the individual (Layer 3).

Layer 1: What's in it for the company?

Layer 2: What's in it for your organization or team?

Layer 3: What's in it for you (the individual)?

Here are examples of Impact Questions that are all open-ended and beg for great follow-up questions:

1   What will the impact be on the overall organization when you make this change?

2   How do you think this decision will influence the performance of your team?

3   When you make this decision, how will this change affect your position? What impact will it have on you, personally, and your day-to-day work?

The following is another example list of Impact Questions asked from big to small. These are essential questions that help you understand where the buyer stands with regard to making the internal business case for the purchase.

1   What impact will this change have on your company's revenue over the next two years?

2   How would you quantify the impact this change could have on your team's win rate this year?

3   What will that percentage increase mean in terms of incremental revenues for fiscal year 20xx?

When you ask what the impact will be for the buyer (stake-holder or decision maker) on a personal level, you'll have in your hands an essential understanding with regard to your ability to influence the buyer's choices. When you understand how a potential change impacts the key stake-holders and decision makers on a personal level, you'll have gained clear insight into the factors that will shape the final decision.

Trade-off Questions

As a seller, you're guiding the buyer through the process of making choices about how to solve their problem. Trade-off Questions help expand and deepen a buyer's thinking about how to envision the problem they're trying to solve and broaden their thinking about the options and trade-offs they can make to solve it.

The best way to think about Trade-off Questions is that you are posing a hypothetical situation that causes the buyer to stop and consider new options. The answers to these questions can also reveal new opportunities with a buyer that hadn't been evident before.

Typical Trade-off Questions start with these phrases:

- "Have you thought about…"
- "What if you…"
- "What would happen if you…"
- "What value would it have if…"
- "Would you rather…"

Here are some general examples of Trade-off Questions:

- "What if you chose to do just X instead of X and Y?"

- "What would happen if you broke this program into two phases?"

- "What value would it have if you started implementation with the sales team before the customer success team instead of the other way around?"

Vision Questions

Vision Questions ask the buyer to envision how they would actually use your product or service. They enable the buyer to take a mental test drive of your solution, to mentally experience the use of your product. They ask the buyer to put themselves in the picture as an owner, or user, and to experience what it would be like to receive their desired value from your product.

Some general examples of Vision Questions are:

- "Walk me through this: How will an engineer on your team use our product in their daily work? In your mind, how will it change their daily work process?"

- "Take me through this: For you personally, what will your day-to-day look like once you're using our product? Take a second and imagine how it will change how you coach your sellers. What would that look like?"

- "Our product generates a lot of operational data you don't currently get. How will you, as the CEO, use this information in your weekly one-on-ones with your department heads?"

As the buyer starts to answer, you'll join in the conversation to help flesh out details of the scenario they are working through.

Vision Questions are less about determining if the buyer's requirements are a match for your product's capabilities and more about aligning your solution with the buyer's vision of the outcomes they want to achieve in the short and long term. In other words, is it helping them achieve their most important thing?

These are high-level questions. Most sellers don't ask them. If you're going for Selling In, you need to demonstrate you have the insight and acumen to help your buyer evaluate their situation in a context more specific than rattling off product specs.

Demonstrations and proof-of-concept pilots are invaluable tools. But, by definition, they are limited in scope. With Vision Questions you enable stakeholders and decision makers to envision the entire experience of using your solution. In the process, you can spot gaps or identify opportunities to make the vision more relevant and compelling.

Insight Questions

Buyers often don't know the answer to an Insight Question, but they probably should.

It's not a gotcha question; the Insight Question is merely one that forces the buyer to stop and think before responding.

➡ If you're going for Selling In, you need to demonstrate you have the **insight and acumen** to help your buyer evaluate their situation.

Insight Questions turbo-charge a conversation, which is a learning experience for both participants. It can take the conversation down paths you hadn't anticipated, opening the door to insight flowing in both directions.

Think about the situation your buyers face. They are inundated with sellers interrogating them with superficial or scripted questions. So, what will it say to the buyer about you, in the context of a competitive sales situation, if you pose a challenging question about their business to which they don't have a ready answer?

It tells them that you are a seller with the insight, value, and experience to help them make good choices and decisions. It would say that you have something to offer them that is different from what other sellers are offering.

For example, in my consulting I've worked with dozens of CEOs to help them improve the productivity of their sales teams. One Insight Question I ask them in our initial conversations is, "Can you tell me how many dollars of revenue each seller on your team is producing per hour of actual selling time?" This question speaks to the heart of seller productivity. Every CEO should know this. And in over twenty years of consulting, not a single CEO ever had the answer. However, every time I've posed the question, it's led to a very productive conversation.

Here's a simple way to come up with your own Insight Questions.

- Talk to your existing customers to discover what is generating the biggest ROI for them from their use of your product. It's common for customers to discover that the source of the greatest ROI from their use of a product is something they hadn't anticipated when they purchased it. It's often driven by a feature or use case that they discovered during implementation that led to unexpected results.

- Make sure you understand what that ROI represents in dollars. Don't guess. Don't assume. Dig into the details with your customer and get the accurate data.

With these data you can build an Insight Question. There's a good probability that some of the other companies you're selling to could similarly profit from the insight you've uncovered from your existing customers. For example, you could say, "We work with a number of similar companies in your field. They've experienced pretty substantial gains in true sales productivity with our solution. Can you tell me how many...?"

Your buyer picks up several signals from this question:

- Companies like theirs are using your product.

- Companies like theirs are experiencing performance improvement using your product.

- This seller has some serious acumen to be asking this question.

- Oh, shit, maybe I am falling behind because I don't know the answer to this question.

The Best Follow-up Questions

There's no question so good that it can't be ruined with a lousy Follow-up Question.

Imagine that you have a scheduled discovery call with a potential buyer. You have your list of the twelve questions you normally ask a buyer during a discovery call. You have been trained to march through all twelve questions in a call. As a result, you're so focused on getting answers to your set questions that you are not really listening. You hear. But you don't process. You don't truly understand the buyer and their concerns.

If you're trying to earn the right to influence a buyer, racing at light speed through your list of standard discovery questions and basically ignoring their answers is not the way to do it.

It's the good Follow-up Question you ask that will inspire the buyer to really open up and provide the in-depth information that leads to a better understanding of their requirements. And here's the key thing to remember: this is not information the buyer just hands out to every seller.

➡ If you're asking great questions, then 100 percent of understanding the answer is **asking the right Follow-up Question.**

If you'll indulge me with a sports metaphor: Questions are like golf. Asking a great question is how you put your ball in the middle of the fairway. Asking a great Follow-up Question is how you knock the ball close to the pin on the green with your second shot. Sticking to your scripted questions is how you hit your tee shot out of bounds.

Follow-up Questions are all about understanding. And listening. You listened carefully to the response to your previous question and knew there was more to be learned. If you're asking great questions, then 100 percent of understanding the answer is asking the right Follow-up Question.

Let's say that you've asked a great question of your buyer. You can tell from the buyer's initial response that this is an important topic for her. You sense that there's more to learn, more information to surface that will guide your decision about the value you should give to influence their choice. You could just ignore your instinct and plunge ahead to the next question you typically ask at this moment. Unfortunately, this is what too many salespeople do. They're so intent on working through their agenda that they don't pay attention to their gut. So the next question they ask is one of their vanilla questions, a scripted question that does nothing to promote a deeper understanding of the buyer and their concerns. That's not good.

Here's what I recommend. Pause for a moment to consider what the buyer just told you and analyze the verbal clues they gave about what they wanted from you next. They left the door open for you to come on in and ask more questions. There's information the buyer wants to provide to help you understand. But she's not going to just give it to you. You have to earn it by asking a great Follow-up Question.

Here are two simply effective Follow-up Questions to ask:

1 "Interesting. Tell me more about that." Okay, it's not really a question. More of a request. But it serves the same purpose. It's saying, "We've only scratched the surface on this topic. I'm curious. Tell me more."

2 "Interesting. And what else can you tell me about this?" This is where you signal the buyer that you sort of understand what they're saying. But clearly, there is more information they have to share about the topic to clarify your understanding. So, what else can they tell you about this to help further your understanding?

You can double down with Follow-up Questions. You can cascade multiple Follow-up Questions together in response to an answer. Just don't overdo it. My recommendation is that you stick with three Follow-up Questions max. After that you start sounding like a little kid following his mom around the house, torturing her with an endless series of whys.

UNDERSTANDING

BEHAVIORAL SCIENTIST KURT Lewin has been quoted as saying, "If you want to truly understand something, try to change it." That's what you do as a seller. You help buyers make a change. Understanding is essential.

In fact, understanding may be the most critical source of value you can provide to your buyers.

Understanding was the reason I won a major eight-figure deal we had no business winning. Especially for a company of our small size. We'd been late to the party. The buyer had been in the market for two years and already winnowed the field of competitors down to their three finalists before I'd even learned that they were looking.

But ten months after I first called the buyer, we closed the deal.

How'd I win? Here's what the customer said: "Out of all the salespeople we spoke to, I felt like you were the only one who really understood what we're trying to accomplish."

Understanding.

As a source of value to your buyers, it's a powerful influencer.

Understanding versus Knowing

"He with the most information wins." It's become a sort of accepted wisdom. In this data age, the person with the most information wins.

There's just one problem with that accepted wisdom. It's dead wrong.

It's not the person with the most information who holds the advantage in any competitive sales situation. The influence advantage belongs to the person who has the best understanding of that information. The one who has the best understanding of the buyer. That's who wins.

There's a big difference between knowing something and truly understanding it. For example, I know that commercial airplanes fly. Having flown close to two million miles in my lifetime, I know a lot about airplanes. I know at a macro level how they fly. But if you were to ask me right now to give you a five-minute extemporaneous speech on the details of Bernoulli's principle and on how jet engines work, I'd quickly show you just how little I understand the details of flight.

So it is with sellers and their buyers. Take your discovery calls for example. The end product of most discovery calls is just a collection of information. "The buyer is having a problem not being able to do X. Their current technology is limited and won't let them do X. They want to do X." Most sellers are satisfied with gathering this superficial level of insight into a buyer.

But what do you actually understand about the buyer with that information?

- Why is not being able to do X a problem for them?

- Is not doing X really the problem? Or is it not being able to grow revenues sufficiently in order to do Y or Z?

- What are the limitations of their existing technology that prevent them from doing X?

- What are the organizational and financial impacts on the buyer of not being able to do X?

- What are the impacts on the stakeholders of not being able to do X?

- What are the impacts on shareholders of the company not hitting its growth goals because it can't do X?

- What would success look like for them if they could do X?

Knowing information is easy. Understanding it takes work.

Here's the thing: as a seller you can't influence your buyer until you understand them. Think about it. What can you influence if you don't truly understand the problem the buyer is trying to solve and the outcomes they want to achieve?

Keep this top of mind: the seller with the best Understanding wins.

Seek First to Understand

"Seek first to understand, then to be understood," Stephen Covey teaches in his *7 Habits of Highly Effective People*. This may be the best sales advice ever. Okay, if not the best, it's certainly in the top five.

The natural instinct of most sellers is to try to persuade before they influence; in other words, they try to sell before they understand. If you want to influence buyer outcomes, you have to approach from a place of Understanding. Understanding builds trust. Understanding builds authority.

Understanding the other party is a fundamental goal of building a functional human connection with anyone. Including your buyers. You want to understand who they are, what they care about, what their needs are, and what's the most important thing to them that you can help them get. You can't do this if you are pushing ahead, trying to persuade without first understanding.

For instance, if you're on a first call with a potential buyer, should your initial objective be to make a thirty-second pitch about the unique qualities of your product that they would be fools not to buy? Or should your goal be to make sure that you begin to understand the needs of the buyer and how you can help that person achieve their desired outcomes?

The only way to truly understand the concerns of another person is to ask them great questions. And then shut up and listen.

You can do all the research you want about your buyer, and you can have read a catalog of personas before you speak with them, but you'll never truly understand them until you ask them some great questions. And then ask some more great questions, all while carefully and deeply listening to what you're being told.

I once closed a large sale with a European telecom company solely through the power of Understanding. I was summoned to present to the managing board of the company. They had narrowed their choices down to two vendors. They wanted to hear a classic bake-off presentation.

I was prepped to present to the twelve suits seated around the conference table. Until I decided not to. I didn't open my laptop, and I didn't present. Instead, I stood in front of the room and outlined on a whiteboard my Understanding of their key challenges and their desired business outcomes from investing in our solution. Step by step, I walked them through their requirements and what their vision of success looked like. At each step I had the board members confirm that I was on the money. I didn't proactively talk about our proposal or product offering at all except to answer some questions that came up while I outlined.

At the end of the meeting, I walked out with the board's commitment to move forward with contract negotiations. I hadn't presented. I'd made them feel understood.

Mini-Guides to Understanding

There are three stages we all mentally pass through when trying to understand something new. These are Exploration, Uncertainty, and Understanding.

When buyers set out to solve a problem or achieve a certain change in their business that requires them to make a purchase decision, they don't spontaneously reach full comprehension of the problem, its solution, or the vendors they could buy from. It takes time and effort to work their way through the stages of Understanding.

At any point in time for any sales opportunity you have in your pipeline, you need to know which stage of Understanding your buyers are currently at. You must be able to separate fact from fiction when you assess just how well you understand your buyer. You need to be ruthlessly realistic about the depth of your understanding of your buyer, their problems, needs, requirements, and desired outcomes. Remember, the seller with the best understanding of the buyer has the influence advantage.

The most effective way I have found to do this is to review every opportunity from both perspectives: that of the buyer and of the seller.

Use the mini-guide below to help you gauge which stage of Understanding the buyer has reached. Step into your buyer's shoes. Look at what's transpired in your sales interactions through their eyes. Then use the criteria for each stage to assess where you think they are in their understanding. Do all of this from their perspective.

The Three Stages of Understanding: Buyer's Perspective

Stage 1: Exploration

"I'm not sure where this is going yet. We don't know what we don't know."

- This is the information and data gathering stage.

- Buyers are trying to define the scope of the problem they need to solve.

- They are gathering ideas about potential possible outcomes and establishing their priorities.

- They have a growing awareness of available solutions, but that is not their focus at this stage.

Stage 2: Uncertainty

"I think I now understand the problem we're trying to solve and the outcomes we can achieve."

- They are gaining a better understanding of their options for solving their problem. However, there are factors at play in terms of potential solutions and business outcomes that the buyer doesn't yet fully understand.

- The buyer is still evaluating their alternatives. They have an idea about what they want to do, but they could still change direction as their understanding develops.

- There is uncertainty about the preference and influence of stakeholders and decision makers. These factors will influence their choice of solution and vendor.

Stage 3: Understanding

"I have the confidence to make my decision."

- Your buyer has worked through all the alternatives with vendors and now has an informed sense of confidence to choose which solution and which vendor to help them achieve their desired outcomes.

- They have completed their internal business case and have quantified the value they can expect to receive from their investment.

- They feel ready to select a solution option and a vendor to work with.

When you've finished assessing the buyer from their point of view, then use the following mini-guide to assess how well you understand the buyer, where they are in their process, and what's left for you to do to close the opportunity and win their business.

The Three Stages of Understanding: Seller's Perspective

Stage 1: Exploration
"I really don't know what's going on yet."

- This is a discovery and data gathering stage.

- Opportunities at this stage haven't earned a spot in your forecast yet.

- Sure, you may have run the BANT rule (Budget, Authority, Need, Timeframe) over the buyer, but that is not enough to truly understand and help them.

Stage 2: Uncertainty
"I think I know what's going on."

- You have to be honest with yourself and admit there are factors at play with key stakeholders and decision makers that you don't yet fully understand. These factors could change the outcome of the deal.

- This stage is frustrating because you want a clear path to success. You want certainty about how you should help the buyer across the finish line, but that understanding hasn't completely materialized.

- Don't rush.

- Be careful: this is where sellers, under pressure from a sales boss trying to convince them they know what is happening on their opportunities, begin making up an internal narrative to convince themselves that they 100 percent understand what's going on. (They don't.)

Stage 3: Understanding
"I have confidence that I know what is going to happen."

- You've worked through all the alternatives with your buyer and feel like you have a firm grasp on what you need to do to win the deal.

- You have an informed sense of confidence about the buyer's decision criteria and what you need to do to help them choose your product.

When you've finished with these quick assessments, you'll have two data points relating to the buyer's level of understanding and your understanding of the buyer. Use these two to triangulate a new location, which is where the buyer really stands in their process. That will give you a more realistic understanding of what's required to help get the buyer across the finish line.

As you can see, arriving at a detailed understanding of your buyer is an essential challenge. You can make it easier to reach that level with a few simple habit changes. Let's dive into the mechanics of how to understand.

Listen to Understand

The single biggest cause of sellers failing to understand their buyers: asking questions of buyers and then listening to respond instead of listening to understand.

It goes like this. A seller asks a question, and then, instead of really listening to the buyer's answer, they think about how they are going to respond to the buyer without first hearing the buyer's answer. They assume they know what the buyer is going to say. The interaction becomes all about them when it should be about the buyer.

There's no point asking great questions of your buyers if you don't make an effort to understand the answers you're given. Similarly, there's no point in wasting your time having a sales conversation with a buyer if you don't understand the questions you are asked, or if you don't understand the information provided by the buyer about the challenge they're trying to solve.

Okay, I can hear the wheels turning. You're thinking, How can I be expected to know the answer to every question the buyer asks? And how can I possibly be knowledgeable enough to understand every answer the buyer provides or to be familiar with every aspect of their business?

You can't. And that's absolutely okay. It's actually the whole point.

Understanding has very little to do with what you know.

If a buyer asks you a question, it's not essential that you know the answer to it on the spot. However, it is absolutely essential that you understand the question and the context of the question they're asking. Why are they asking the question? Why is it important to them? What are they trying to develop an understanding of? Without this understanding, how can you possibly provide the most appropriate answer and information in reply?

In other words, you can't give good value to your buyer if you don't first understand the context and motivation for the information they want from you and the trade-offs and choices they have to make. This requires you to persist in asking questions and listening until you can confirm that you understand.

The question is, how should you be listening?

Hearing versus Listening

Hearing and listening are very different actions. *Hearing* is an involuntary process that detects noise (or vibrations). *Listening* is a voluntary action you take to make sense of the noises you hear.

Think back to a sales call you were on. Perhaps you were a little distracted. Maybe you were bored because this prospect seemed just like every other you'd talked to. Or possibly you made some judgment about the buyer based on their LinkedIn profile and decided that they weren't a serious prospect.

You asked the buyer a question, and you heard their answer. But for whatever reason, you didn't actually *listen* to that response. You made a note of what you remembered they said. And then you plunged ahead with your next question. The buyer may have communicated some significant information that you should have pursued. You heard it. But didn't listen.

When you say "I hear you" to someone to acknowledge what they've told you, what you're really saying is, "Yeah, I registered that there were noises coming out of your mouth, but I wasn't actually listening." Unfortunately, this is too common an occurrence in our lives. We perpetuate the myth that we are all so busy that we don't have time to listen.

But the opposite is true. We are all so busy because we don't take the time to listen. As a result, we're slowing everything down because we force people to repeat what they've told us before.

Want to speed things up? Listen carefully; listen slowly.

Listening Slowly

The Greek Stoic philosopher Epictetus wrote that we should take a moment before we react to provocations. In other words, when we are listening to another person speak, we should pause to collect ourselves to reduce the temptation to react impulsively. And to avoid saying something we might later regret.

This is especially important if you're trying to influence a buyer.

Which is where patience enters the picture.

Slowing your roll a bit forces you to think, not react. It gives you the time to challenge your internal assumptions that you understood exactly what the buyer meant with their question instead of rushing to give them a hasty, ill-considered answer.

So how do you slow down your listening?

Listen with a pause.

A young salesperson approached me after a workshop I'd conducted and said he was having a listening problem. He was relatively new at his job. He loved his work. He was excited to help his customers. However, he often found that he was so distracted thinking about what his answers were going to be during a call that he didn't really listen to his buyer's questions.

Look, I know you want to impress the buyer and show off what you know. It's understandable. Just don't jump the gun. Give yourself a chance to process what you hear and really listen to understand what the other person is saying to you before you respond.

- Pause before you respond to a question.

- Pause before you respond to an answer with another question.

- Physically pause. Take a sec. Process what you just heard.

Here's a simple technique you can use to make a habit of listening slowly: Give yourself a "one Mississippi" count before responding. Take a physical break before you respond to a buyer's question or their response to a question you asked. It's as easy as it sounds. Just stop, take a breath, and count "one Mississippi" before you respond to a buyer question or answer. (Do I need to tell you to say it silently to yourself?) This will barely take a second.

It doesn't have to be a deep, cleansing breath like you do in yoga. It definitely doesn't need to be audible. Just take a breath in. *One Mississippi.* By building in this pause, you're allowing yourself a little head space to consolidate what you just heard from the buyer, enabling you to formulate a thoughtful response instead of reacting to bait.

The person you're speaking with won't notice the pause. They will notice, however, the difference in the value of the questions you ask and the responses you give to their questions.

What Are We Missing?

Asking reflection questions is an easy Understanding habit to develop. However, by itself it has its limits.

You can use reflection questions to help make sure you don't proceed to your next question until you understand the buyer's answer. You also utilize them to make sure you understand a question the buyer asked before you attempt to answer it.

Here are just a few examples:

- "What I heard you say was [this]. Is that correct?"

- "I want to make sure I understand this correctly. You said..."

- "So, your understanding is this... Did I get that right?"

The limitation of reflection questions is that they are based on an assumption that the buyer has a full understanding of whatever you're asking them to confirm. That's a dangerous assumption to make. Instead of using a reflection question to confirm your understanding of your buyer's perspective on a certain topic, use it to challenge the buyer's understanding.

"What I heard you say was [this]. What are we missing?"

Buyers generally appreciate sellers who take the time to clarify their understanding of a buyer's question or statement.

Here's the value to reflection: it makes you slow down. Sometimes we get a bit too excited in sales. You get in a hurry to move a deal forward, and your biases start to kick in. You assume you know what a buyer is going to say to you.

Reflection forces you to listen slowly because it inserts a natural pause into how you listen. Use it. Take advantage of it.

CHAPTER

12

GENEROSITY

GENEROSITY. IT'S NOT a word that's generally associated with sales. It should be.

This chapter will further disrupt your understanding of how to sell. After all, when have you ever had someone tell you that generosity is one of the core factors that builds consistent sales success? Probably never. Until now.

You've heard of *buyer-centric* selling, right? It's one of the more commonly mentioned, and least utilized, modes of selling. I mean, the idea makes perfect sense: Place the buyer at the center of your sales efforts. Align how you sell with how the buyer buys. It's something we should all aspire to do.

However, for most sellers, buyer-centric selling falls victim to the demands of the archaic, linear, stage-based sales processes that they've been trained to follow. The processes in which the buyer is merely an inconvenient obstacle that stands in the way of their getting an order. Sound familiar?

Let's try something better. A new perspective to add to your selling.

Selling, when done well, is an act of Generosity.

If the prime objective of Selling In is to listen to understand what the most important thing is to your buyer and then help them get it, then Selling In is, at heart, an act of Generosity. It's about being selfless and giving, helping others get what is most important to them.

I operate with the mindset that I can succeed only to the extent that I help my buyers get what is most important to them. That's Generosity. That's Selling In. You listen (generous) to define and understand (generous) what is most important to your buyer (generous) and help them get it (generous).

So far in this book you've learned how to

- form a durable human Connection with your buyer;

- use your Curiosity to demonstrate a genuine interest in how you can help them; and

- invest your time to help your buyer, as well as you, develop a full Understanding of their problems and desired outcomes.

Now you're going to learn how to deploy your Generosity to enable your buyers with the value and vision they need to make informed trade-offs, choices, and decisions.

Generosity Is Good for Your Soul . . . and Wallet

Words matter. They shape your perspective on the things you do and how you feel about them. Generosity is one of those words for sellers. Being generous makes you feel better about yourself and what you do.

Being generous is innate human behavior. Yet, despite the value it has for both your buyers and you, generosity is perceived as a weakness by many sales bosses and sales trainers. It's not salesy enough. It's sacrificed on the altar of expediency. "Don't be a giver. Be a closer."

That's just crazy talk. On many levels.

Here's the thing. Being generous is good for your mental health. It's a hedge against the very real risk of burnout that many sellers experience. Psychologists believe that even though you are being generous for the benefit of others, Generosity increases your personal sense of well-being.[10]

Generosity is also a trigger for reciprocity. When you give something of actual value to your buyers, you make it more likely that they will give something to you. This feels good. It makes the areas of your brain associated with social connection and trust light up, which makes you want to give again.

The key to successful giving? Understanding. As humans we want to believe that the value we give to our buyers will be perceived by them to have actual value. The more you truly understand your buyer's problem, truly understand what the most important thing is to them, and truly understand how the value you're providing will help them achieve that, the better giving will feel to you.

Having a positive impact on the lives of others is its own reward. And it's also the path to winning more deals and the tangible and intangible rewards that brings.

So, just in case you still need another reason to stop Selling Out, this is it. The Sell In Pillars (Connection, Curiosity, Understanding, Generosity) make you feel better about yourself and the work you do.

Being a Good Giver Is Good

Giving has an undeserved bad rap in sales. I sat through a presentation at a major sales conference during which a prominent analyst claimed that being a giver in sales was de facto bad. And you know what? He wasn't wrong. But he wasn't right, either.

Let's break this down so you understand the importance of being appropriately generous with the value you give to your buyers.

In his book *Give and Take*, Adam Grant wrote that in our relationships at work we all fall into one of four categories: Good Givers, Matchers, Takers, and Bad Givers. (Grant is much more nuanced in his descriptions of givers. Hopefully, he'll forgive me my simplification.)

He cited research that stack ranked the performance of each of these giver types. I'll summarize these from worst to first.

Bad Givers are the least productive. Bad Givers are sellers who are people pleasers. They never connect with or understand what is most important to the buyer. So they resort to unrestrained giving as a weak substitute for that understanding in the faint hope that something they give will resonate with the buyer. This is the "show up and throw up" seller. Bad Givers are Selling Out.

Next to the worst are **Takers**. Takers are the self-interested sellers who look at buyers solely through the lens of what the buyer can do for them. They pitch and sell before they understand. They resort to manipulation tactics in an effort to control their buyers and the pace of their buying. Takers are garden variety persuasion pushers. Takers are Selling Out.

Next up are **Matchers**. Matchers see sales as a quid pro quo kind of deal. Matchers match the value of what they give to buyers to the value of what they receive in return. Matchers believe in the fiction that buying is a well-ordered process they can control by how and when they give to their buyers. Matchers are Selling Out.

Good Givers top the list. These are sellers who are equally buyer-centric and self-interested. They are sellers with an agenda. "If I can help my buyer get the thing that is most important to them, then I will reap the psychological and financial rewards that are important to me." Good Givers are transparent with their buyers about their giving agenda, which builds trust and tightens the alignment between seller and the buyer. Good Givers are Selling In.

In case I wasn't clear: you want to be a Good Giver. Grant and others have found that people are most successful when they are motivated both by helping others and by being successful. They are equally selfless and self-motivated. This applies to you as a seller too.

The buyer's experience with you should instill in them the feeling that your most important thing is helping them to get their most important thing. You do well by doing good.

Uh, What Is Giving Value?

When you're Selling In, your Generosity flows from giving your buyers value and vision. So, here's the big question for you. What is *value*?

Value is one of the most overused and least well-defined terms in sales. The word is used so casually that it practically has no meaning. Every sales leader and salesperson talks about adding value, creating value, or delivering value to the buyer without precisely understanding what it means.

But it sure sounds good, right?

The problem is that in sales, *value* is typically defined by the seller, which is pointless. Like beauty, value is in the eye of the beholder; only the buyer can decide what's of value to them.

So, how does a buyer decide what's of value in their buying process? Let's keep it simple because it's easy to over-complicate the definition of value.

A buyer's decision-making process has a beginning and an end. During the course of their buying journey, they are going to give you a limited number of opportunities to interact with them. Therefore, you need to make each sales interaction count. What does that mean? The result of every single sales interaction you have with a buyer must be that you have helped the buyer move closer to making their choice. Even if by only a small amount. Even a tiny step. You achieve this by giving good value.

Okay, so what's value to a buyer?

VALUE = PROGRESS

To give good value to a buyer simply means that your buyer is closer to making their choice at the end of an interaction with you than they were at the beginning. In other words, buyers measure value by progress. Are they closer to making a decision about your solution? Are they closer to making a decision about you and their buying experience?

Whatever you shared with them that enabled them to make this progress constitutes value. This value can be in any shape or form. It could be a question. Or a piece of content. Or a demo. Or a presentation. Or a commercial insight. The form of the value you give doesn't matter. The only thing that matters is how your buyer receives and perceives the value.

One simple example of value could be making a strong first impression. Making your buyer feel comfortable with you is a form of value for them.

Another example is asking an Insight Question about something your buyer should know about their business but don't, something that forces them to think differently about the challenge they're trying to address. That has value for them.

Most critically, understanding the buyer and what the most important thing is to them, making them feel understood, is a massive source of value for the buyer. (Why would they continue to invest their time with a seller that they feel doesn't understand them? They won't.) So, good questions with great follow-up and reflective questions to confirm your understanding also have value for buyers.

Sources of Value

Value can be tangible. Value can be intangible. Tangible sources of value tend to impact and influence the buyer's decision about your solution (product or service). Intangible sources of value tend to impact and influence the buyer's buying experience and their decision about you (i.e., "Why you?").

What follows are some examples of tangible and intangible value.

SOURCES OF TANGIBLE VALUE

Asking a great question

Asking a great Follow-Up Question

A new perspective based on technology changes

A new perspective based on industry changes

A strong customer review

A key piece of relevant content

A customer case study

An analyst report

Research data

An ROI analysis and business case

The buyer's Vision of Success

SOURCES OF INTANGIBLE VALUE
Understanding the buyer's most important thing
Building trust
Strong personal connections with key stakeholders
Your responsiveness
Your Generosity
Making your buyer feel heard and understood
The buyer's Vision of Success
A positive ROTA on your interactions
Persistent Curiosity
First impressions
The buying experience

In reality, the form of your value doesn't matter. All that matters is how it is perceived and received by your buyer.

What doesn't have value for your buyers?

- Being salesy
- Pitching

- Selling before you understand
- Pushy persuasion
- Superficial scripted questions
- Being a know-it-all

In short, Selling Out has no value for your buyers.

The bottom line: the value you give to your buyer has to help them move closer to making their choice about you after your interaction with them. In other words, did your value help them make progress?

Effective Giving Requires a Plan

Value doesn't just materialize by accident. Giving good value is a deliberate sales action.

Remember, you have only a limited number of chances to interact with your buyer on each sales opportunity. Each one is important and has to be carefully thought through.

As a rule, for anything you provide to the buyer to be of value, it must empower them to be closer to making their choice after receiving it than they were before. This is not necessarily a high bar to hurdle, but it requires intent and planning.

Giving good value is intentional. It usually doesn't happen by accident. It requires that you have a simple value plan for every sales interaction. No matter how big (an in-person meeting) or how small (an email) the interaction, it requires a value plan before you execute it. Don't be put off by the word *plan*. It just means that you have to be intentional about the value you provide.

Here's a simple and effective way to build your value plan. Before an interaction with a buyer, answer these three questions:

1 What value does the buyer need from me now to make progress and move closer to making their choice?

2 How and why will the value I provide enable the buyer to make progress and move closer to making their choice?

3 What commitments will the buyer make in exchange for receiving this value?

I suggest you write your answers down. It will really help you think through your intention for each and every sales touch.

You must know the answers to these questions before each sales interaction. What value does my buyer need from me now to move closer to making their choice? What will they do in exchange for receiving this value? The answers will necessarily change based on where the buyer sits in their decision-making process. However, you absolutely must know the answers at all times for every qualified opportunity in your pipeline.

This is big. If you don't know the answers to these, then stop. Don't take any action until you can answer these questions. Don't send an email. Don't call. Don't "check in" in any way. Take your hands off your keyboard and slowly back away from your computer.

The last thing you want to do in the midst of a buying journey is consume a buyer's time and attention without giving them something of value in return. You might get away with it once. Twice, maybe. More than that, and they'll reasonably conclude that you aren't worth the additional investment, and they will stop giving you their time and attention.

The better choice is always to do nothing if you don't have a ready answer to those questions. In fact, being unable to answer them is a sign that you need to go back and use your Curiosity and Understanding to do some more digging with your buyer, right? Having an actual understanding of what the buyer needs from you to move closer to making a decision about you flows from asking great questions and listening slowly to make sure you understand the answers.

Non-obvious Sources of Value

You are no doubt familiar with the traditional and more obvious sources of value you can give to your buyers, which I outlined earlier. Every seller is somewhat familiar with those.

However, there are some non-obvious sources of value that exert equal, if not greater, sway over the decisions of your buyers. The Selling In seller prioritizes these sources of value because these are things that are under their direct control.

Maximize Your Buyer's Return on Time and Attention

What's your buyer's return on time and attention (ROTA) in you?

In sales, you are part of the noise. You are just one more channel of information vying for your distracted buyer's attention. And despite what you've read about how difficult it is to capture the attention of your buyers via email, social media, or phone, that's not the real challenge. The hard part is keeping the attention of your buyers once you have it. You have to continuously prove that you are worth your buyer's investment of time.

This is the unwritten contract in sales between you, the seller, and your buyers. When your buyer invests some of their time in you, you have to give them something of value in return.

We all calculate this ROTA. One time, I walked into a bicycle shop looking for more information on a brand of road bike that was on display in their front window. I was

➡ Great questions are more **powerful influencers** than any statements of fact you can make.

in the market. I was the only customer in the store. After I'd spent about five minutes examining the display bike, a salesperson still hadn't bothered to come around from behind the checkout counter to talk to me. That was not a good return on my time and attention. I left and bought the same bike elsewhere.

An absence of ROTA is why a first call doesn't turn into a second call. Or a second call into a third.

Think back to opportunities you've worked on that went silent. Perhaps the buyer ghosted you. They're not ignoring you. They've made a decision about you. You weren't a good use of their time. And they've forgotten you. That's the impact of Selling Out.

Persistent Curiosity

When momentum on a sales opportunity starts to stall, it's usually for one of two reasons.

1   The buyer has questions that need to be answered before they can move forward in their process. They're stuck at the uncertainty stage of Understanding.

2   You're stuck at the uncertainty stage. You don't know what you should do next to help the buyer make progress.

The only solution to a lack of understanding is more Curiosity. You need to persist and ask more questions to determine what is missing from the understanding of the buyer. Cranking up your Curiosity is a good way to give more value to your buyer.

This type of persistent Curiosity elevates a buyer's perception of your value. And it opens the door wider to your influence.

However, I do frequently get asked this question: Is it possible to ask too many questions?

If all you're going to do is interrogate the buyer with superficial scripted questions, then all bets are off. That is the opposite of persistent Curiosity. That's intellectually lazy. However, if you're asking relevant questions, like any of the six types of questions from Chapter 10 on Curiosity, then the only limitation on the number of questions you can ask is the amount of time and attention the buyer has available for answers.

Remember: great questions are more powerful influencers than any statements of fact you can make.

Accelerated Responsiveness

Being responsive is one of the most powerful sources of value that's under your complete control. If you do it right, it creates a positive perception in the mind of your buyers of what it will be like to do business with you and your company.

Responsiveness is not about being fast. It's about enabling forward progress for the buyer. It's about compressing timeframes. It's about managing expectations. It's about creating a positive buying experience.

Here are a few incredibly powerful ways to accelerate your responsiveness:

Prioritize responding to all messages from active opportunities

We're all busy. Inboxes are full. Message channels are overflowing. And your buyers don't care. They reached out to you for a reason. They need something from you, and they don't want to wait. Make it a priority to respond.

In my career, I've experienced a direct correlation between my responsiveness and my win rate. You will too.

Eliminate wasted days between sales interactions

Don't inadvertently add days into the buyer's decision timeline. It's typical for a seller to send content to a buyer and then suggest that they'll follow up the next week. Why? Are you sending them a two-hundred-page tome? Or something that takes fifteen minutes to read?

Pro tip: Always propose a time for a follow-up call the *next business day*. I like to trigger their curiosity by saying something like, "There are two key points in this content that directly relate to the trade-offs you're evaluating. Would you be open to a discussion about these tomorrow at three?"

Manage buyer expectations

If you can't provide an immediate answer to a question a buyer asked during a call or in a message to you, quickly determine how long it will take to respond. Then immediately message the buyer to set an expectation for when you will respond with the information they need.

Live up to your commitments

If you promise a response at a certain date and time, move heaven and earth to make it happen. Remember the MICE acronym for building trust? E is for execution, or living up to your commitments. There aren't a ton of opportunities in pre-sales to demonstrate that you can reliably meet your commitments. This is an easy and effective way to do that. Don't blow it.

Selling Out means not paying attention to the impact your actions have on the buyer's perception of you. Being responsive is one of the most effective methods to influence that.

—

Is Your Value Valuable?

Remember that a majority of the buying decision is based on your buyer's experience with you.

With the understanding that you can never know exactly what your buyers are thinking about you, you need to ask their opinion of how you're doing.

If you're on a call and the buyer asks you a question, give your response and then ask, "Was this helpful? Did I fully answer your question?" It's the same if you answer a question in a message or email.

The point of doing this is not to stroke your ego. It's to confirm with the buyer that the value you provided helped them better understand how they're going to use your product. Or made clear the value they'll receive from using it. In other words, make sure they really understand how your product will be used on a day-to-day basis within their organization (or outside the organization by external users) and the impact it will have in achieving their desired business outcomes. Ask: "Is it clear how your account executives will use this feature and integrate it into their daily sales process?"

Pro tip: Always send the buyer a written confirmation or summary of the buyer's answers to these questions. Ask them to correct you if you summarized something incorrectly. That becomes a useful trigger for additional questions, discovery, and understanding.

Give Your Buyers a Compelling Vision of Success

Here's a question for you. At that moment when your buyers make their final choice and purchase decision, what are they actually buying?

It's not your product or service. What they're actually deciding to buy is a vision of the outcomes they'll achieve using your product. A vision of the value they'll receive from achieving those outcomes. A vision of the ROI they'll earn.

Where do they get that vision?

From you.

There's one story that you, as a seller, must be able to tell. It's the story that paints the vision of what success will look like for your buyer in using your product to achieve their most important thing.

John Steinbeck, the great American novelist, captured it best when he wrote in *East of Eden*, "If a story is not about the hearer, he will not listen... The strange and foreign is not interesting—only the deeply personal and familiar."

In short, the story your buyer most wants to hear is their own. A story in which they are the hero who overcomes formidable obstacles to slay the dragon and bring peace to the kingdom. In other words, the story in which they solve their business problem and achieve the thing that is most important to them.

This is the buyer's Vision of Success.

This is the compelling story that triggers a purchase decision. This is the story that enables buyers to put themselves into the picture and emotionally experience what success will feel like. It's the vision of the outcomes their organization will achieve using your product, and what that success will mean for them personally.

This is the story they want to tell themselves: one story for all the stakeholders and decision makers involved that becomes the single source of truth for their decision-making. Meaning that if someone questions the decision, then the Vision of Success is used to justify the rationale for the purchase.

Creating the Buyer's Vision of Success

The buyer's Vision of Success is not a story you make up. It's one you co-create with your buyer at every step of their buying journey. Every question you ask, every answer you provide, every insight and piece of content you share should be framed in the context of helping shape your buyer's vision of ultimate success.

The vision assumes a more recognizable shape as it grows. It starts with a broad point of view and becomes increasingly specific as you help the buyer define their problem and narrow their focus on the various available options to achieve their desired outcomes.

Researchers have determined that people who are contemplating making a change, which is exactly what the act of buying is, go through a number of mental steps.[11] One of the main steps that every person undertakes is key to building the Vision of Success and what I call the *mental test drive*.

Every time anyone makes a purchase decision, they first create a detailed mental image of what it would be like to use the product. In that image, they picture themselves enjoying the value of the product they are purchasing. This is the mental test drive. We all do it.

Imagine that you are going to buy or lease a new car. You visit the manufacturer's website. You scan through glossy photos of cars and read about the particular model you're interested in. As you browse, you catch yourself picturing what it would be like to be behind the wheel of the car, maybe driving on winding roads through the mountains to get to your favorite hiking spot or cruising on a cloudless day along the beach with the sunroof open to your favorite surf break. That's the mental test drive.

Similarly, your buyers want to physically sample the experience of achieving their desired business outcomes with your product or service. However, that's not always possible. Which means you need to take them on mental test drives of your solution. In order to build a Vision of

Success that is embraced by the buyer, you need to ask questions that trigger the buyer to take that mental test drive of your product. (Refer to Chapter 10 to refresh your memory about Vision Questions.)

Here's an example: "I asked you before what you thought the performance improvement you'd get from our product would be. You said you thought you'd see a 10 percent productivity improvement. So, tell me how you see that working. Let's use Joni in marketing as an example. Walk me through Joni's daily process and tell me how her productivity would improve as a result of using our system."

What happens here is, the buyer has to think through the practical implications of using your product and the way it would affect specific details of her and her team's daily work. In other words, she has to take your product on a mental test drive.

These detailed mental test drives are one of the most effective ways you can help buyers make sense of the information they've gathered and the value you've been sharing with them. They mentally work through various scenarios with your solution that they have only assumed before, which helps them recognize unexpected upsides or spot potential pitfalls. It helps them move from Uncertainty to Understanding.

In addition, mental test drives are an emotional trigger because they require the buyer to center themselves in the scenario. At that point, buyers start feeling a sense of ownership of the story and how it eventually turns out.

Six Elements of Building an Effective Buyer's Vision of Success

1   Record all understandings in a shared document
Create a shared document in which you and the buyer collaborate to build their Vision of Success as you move through their buying journey. This document gives your buyer an understanding of their story all in one place. Every time they review it, they are creating a more concrete vision of what success will look like for them after they buy from you. That has real value for your buyers.

At the start of every sales call, take two minutes to screenshare the vision doc and quickly recap the understandings that are contained therein. Confirm that you're still in alignment. If not, be prepared to dig in with more questions to understand what has changed.

2   Align on a definition of success
Confirm that your Vision of Success for your buyer is aligned with their own. This will be documented in the shared vision doc.

3   Take the buyer on a lot of mental test drives
Each mental test drive is a building block of the Vision of

Success. Walk the buyer through as many detailed scenarios as you can about the use of product or service. Each mental test drive deepens the buyer's understanding of your solution.

4 Document the outcomes of mental test drives

After every sales interaction, verbally confirm with the buyer your understanding about what they learned and the outcome of the mental test drive. Then update the shared vision doc with this understanding.

5 Quantify the dollar impact of the vision

A Vision of Success isn't complete if the value of success hasn't been quantified in dollars. Every story needs to have an ending. In this case, the ending has to be spelled out financially. For instance, if one of the signposts of success for your buyer will be a 5 percent increase in revenue, what does that mean for them in terms of dollars?

Quantifying the impact is so important because it means that the buyer has done, or is in the process of doing, their internal business case for the transformation, change, or investment that you're proposing. That's the ultimate mental test drive. That means that when you complete their vision, the buyer will be in a position to quickly act.

6 Be first with the vision

This is the pot of gold at the end of the Vision of Success rainbow.

A study of B2B buyers found that their buying into a Vision of Success correlated with a 65 percent probability of their awarding the vendor with their business. Those are great odds that any seller should jump at achieving. It also suggests that you want to be the first seller to get buy-in from the buyer on your Vision of Success for them.

What's the key for being first with your vision? Understanding. Being the first seller to understand the buyer, the nature and scope of their problem, and their most important thing. A successful Vision of Success is never built on assumptions.

This means building a trust-based Connection with your buyer, using your empathy and Curiosity to discover and develop a true Understanding of the most important thing they need your help to get, and then supporting them with your Generosity by enabling them to visualize the value they would receive from successfully using your product or service.

CHAPTER
13

THE "SECRET" SALES ACCELERATOR

SALES ACCELERATION. IT'S a myth. It's also the holy grail for sellers. Everyone is seeking the path to enlightenment that will reveal the secret of how to rush a buyer through their sales funnel at a higher velocity. Many claim that they possess "secret knowledge" that magically accelerates sales. They don't—for the simple reason that such knowledge doesn't exist.

Let's set aside the discounts and other financial goodies that sellers offer buyers to induce them to sign an order earlier than they had planned. That's not sales acceleration. For the most part, that's just bad business. It's like handing a wad of cash to a buyer, offering a big discount, effectively bribing them to pull an order from July into June just so your sales bosses can hit their targets.

In general, talk of sales acceleration is self-indulgent myth-making by authors and sales tech vendors who want you to believe that you can manipulate and control the actions of your buyers. Which you can't. Of course, there are the rare exceptions; they're what keeps the myth alive.

As I've shared throughout this book, the only things that you can actually control in sales are the actions you take. That's Selling In. When you're Selling In, you will have better and more productive conversations with your buyers. You will close more opportunities because you'll have a better understanding of what your buyers want, what success means for them, and what they need from you to make their decision.

However, there's a hidden bonus when you're Selling In. You can experience a kind of trampoline effect, a quasi-sales accelerator, that actually enables your buyers to make their decision sooner than they had planned. Meaning that you'll help your buyers achieve their strategic objective of quickly gathering and making sense of the information they need to make their purchase decision with the least possible investment of their time, attention, and resources.

I've experienced the trampoline effect of Selling In many, many times in my sales career. In fact, it shaped how I sold. I learned that being the first seller to reach certain key milestones with the buyer would often lead to an unexpectedly fast decision in my favor.

The first time I experienced this was on a highly competitive deal that I won before the buyer had even asked for a formal proposal. I was surprised. At first, I thought that bringing the decision forward a couple months was due to my superior sales abilities. Yeah, well, not really. What actually happened was the buyer made the kind of rational purchase decision that customers routinely make all the time without sellers even being aware of it. However, once you understand why and how buyers make this type of decision, you'll see why Selling In is so valuable.

So, what is this "secret" decision that buyers make?

It's the Good Enough Decision.

And it's the type of decision your buyers make. All. The. Time.

The Good Enough Decision

Did I just say that buyers make rational decisions? Yes, I did. Oftentimes the decisions your buyers make are rational, not emotional or logical.

I know—you're shocked. You've no doubt read or been trained to believe that your buyers' decision-making is based on emotions and justified after the fact with logic. And perhaps you've lost a deal where you just knew that your product was a better fit for the buyer than the one they chose. You think to yourself, "That's just not a rational decision."

Actually, it probably was. Look, there's no denying that decisions are informed by emotion and logic. But from the perspective of the buyer, their decisions are rational.

Understanding this distinction gives you an essential advantage in winning more deals.

Let me quickly walk you through this. It's so simple and, well, rational. A person's ability to make the "best" decision about how to solve a problem, like which product to purchase to achieve a desired outcome, is limited by three constraints:

1 Time

2 Information

3 Understanding

These constraints were articulated by Nobel Prize–winning economist Herbert Simon, who developed the philosophy of bounded rationality. He found that an individual's, or an organization's, ability to make an optimally rational decision about anything would always be compromised by these three constraints.

> **Time:** No buyer has unlimited time to devote to making a purchase decision. No matter how important the decision is to the company or individual, they can't devote unlimited resources (i.e., time and attention) to the task.

Information: Your buyer does not have unlimited access to perfect information about their problem and potential solutions. Despite your experience and expertise, and as good as your content may be, the buyer will always have unanswered questions about your product and how it will help them achieve their desired outcomes.

Understanding: Your buyer will never have a perfect understanding of the scope and impact of the problem they are trying to solve. Nor will they ever have a perfect understanding of the outcomes they can achieve, and the value they can receive, from using your product. There will always be unknowns associated with factors such as risk and the probability of success.

So, what type of decision do your buyers make when faced with these constraints? One that is *good enough*.

Given the three decision constraints, the path that most buyers follow when making a decision is to make what Simon termed a *satisficed* choice. Satisfice is a conjoining of the words *satisfy* and *suffice*.

Your buyers don't have access to perfect information; they don't have the time to develop a perfect understanding of their problem, their desired outcomes, or the possible solutions; and they generally don't have the time and resources to evaluate every single option or alternative available to them.

So, when they identify a solution that both satisfies their requirements to solve their problems and sufficiently achieves their desired outcomes, they stop looking at other options and make their decision. They pull the plug on their buying journey.

Here are the buyer's rationales for making the satisficed decision.

- "We've identified and chosen a solution that satisfies our requirements for solving our problem and is sufficient to achieve our desired business outcomes."

- "We could invest more of our time, attention, and resources to keep evaluating additional solutions. However, we don't believe we'll find anything that is significantly better than our choice."

- "We've decided that any marginal return we could get from investing more of our time, attention, and resources in evaluating additional solution options isn't worthwhile. This choice is good enough."

That's a rational decision.

Buyers don't believe that investing another day, week, or month to further investigate other solutions will yield a substantially better outcome than the satisficed one. So, they declare victory and move on to the next project that needs their time and attention.

What's the compelling event that causes the buyer to make the satisficed choice or Good Enough Decision? Achieving a Stage 3: Understanding level of your solution and how it satisfices for all of their requirements.

The Vision of Success you create for the buyer is often a trigger for their Good Enough Decision. You've confirmed that your solution meets their requirements and will enable them to achieve what is most important to them. (Or, at a minimum, what you provide is closer to meeting their requirements than anything else they've evaluated so far.)

As previously noted, the first seller to present a Vision of Success that satisfies the buyer's requirements and suffices in enabling them to achieve their most important thing (i.e., satisfices) stands the best chance of winning. A 65 percent chance. These are good odds; as a seller, you want that probability of winning.

However, the Vision of Success is not the only decision trigger. The buyer could reach Stage 3: Understanding at any point based on your questions, your understanding, and the value you've given. This is why the Sell In Pillars are incredibly valuable and important milestones to achieve—they signify that the buyer is making progress toward Understanding. And toward making their Good Enough Decision.

Be First to the Pillars

Here's the question: What thing, or things, have to occur for you to be in a position to be the first seller to present a Vision of Success that satisfices for your buyer? Well, you have to be first in a number of areas, which the pillars enable you to do. In reverse order, you have to be:

The first to Understanding. You can't create a relevant and compelling Vision of Success if you don't have a detailed and accurate understanding of the problem the buyer wants to solve, their desired outcome, and their most important thing. Being the first seller to make your buyer feel understood is a decisive competitive advantage.

The first to Curiosity. To be the first to Understanding, you need information from your buyer. There's a direct link from the quality of the questions you ask to the depth of information the buyer will share with you. Being the first seller to ask great questions that require the buyer to think before answering is a solid differentiator.

The first to credibility and trust. There's also a direct link between the quality of the information the buyer will share and the level of credibility and trust you've earned with them. To be the first to credibility and trust is a game changer. It opens a window of insight into the buyer and their most important thing that might otherwise remain closed to you. Having access to more insight into the buyer that can be converted into Understanding can effectively knock competitors out of the game.

The first to answer "Why you?" The path to trust, Curiosity, Understanding, and Generosity runs through the "Why you" question: without a positive answer to it, your opportunities never get out of first gear. And "Why you?" never gets asked without first having a human connection with the buyer.

The first to Connection. This is the most elemental part of sales. Nothing happens without a human connection. The buyer, whether it's a single decision maker or a flock of stakeholders, forms a lasting perception of you from the moment of your first contact as a human and as a resource to help them understand and get their most important thing. Your ability to win an opportunity can, and will, turn on that initial moment with a buyer. Everything that follows in your sales process flows through Connection. Being the first seller to achieve all the milestones listed above depends on it.

—

BEING THE first seller to these milestones enables your buyers to accelerate their decision cycles as well. It's a decision accelerator. Unlike sales acceleration, decision acceleration is real—and you can make it happen.

It all starts with that decisive first moment with your buyer. Do they perceive that you are Selling In? Or Selling Out?

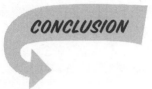

CONCLUSION

DON'T BE A
SALES ZOMBIE

"I THINK HOLLYWOOD'S CONTINUING fascination with zombies comes from the fact that there are so many of them among us. They look the same, they sound the same, but they've been unplugged. The thing that made us want to look at them, listen to them: it's gone. They're still here, but they're just waiting to be embalmed."[12]

When I first read this paragraph from Timothy Hallinan's novel, I thought the author was describing the typical salesperson.

Think about it for a second.

We all know sellers that look the same and sound the same as they always have. Yet there's something different about them. An emptiness. A stillness. They've come unplugged. They've stopped learning. They've stopped improving. The things that made them interesting to buyers, and that made buyers want to listen to them, have vanished.

Every day they show up for work. But they're not connected to the real world around them. They've burned out.

They're Selling Out. They've become . . . sales zombies.

That's the salesy seller.

Who pitches before connecting.

Who tells instead of asks.

Who sells before they understand.

Who persuades instead of influences.

Who's become someone even the seller themself doesn't recognize. Just blindly following a process wherever it goes, without a plan of their own to improve or deliver.

As you've learned, it doesn't have to be this way. You can seize control over how you sell. Not only can you; you have to. Sellout zombies never change. But you are different. You can choose to take action. And make an immediate difference.

By Selling In.

Make authentic human connections with your buyers.

Develop greater credibility and trust.

Unlock doors with your curiosity.

Make your buyer feel heard and understood.

Give generously of your value and vision to help the buyer get what is most important to them.

There is not just one way to sell. Those who are Selling In are creating their own way with a blend of values, character, technique, methods, and process.

This is the ultimate step to success in sales on your own terms.

Selling In. It's your ticket to the career of your choice. And to the life of your choice.

Selling Out. It's your ticket to a career in a different profession.

It's your choice which type of seller you want to become.

ACKNOWLEDGMENTS

JUST AS NO one wins a sale on their own, no one writes a book alone. Like sales, writing is a team sport.

Let's start with the biggest part of the team. That's you, the reader. The inspiration for this book came from you. The millions of you who have listened to my thousand-plus podcast episodes, or who have followed my posts on LinkedIn and purchased my books. What I've learned from my interactions with you is that despite being inundated with innovative sales tech and data, you crave a more authentically human way to effectively connect with your buyers and help them make decisions. This book is the answer to that desire.

I'm incredibly grateful to the managers in the early years of my career who put up with me. I'm not easy. They hired me into roles that I was unqualified to fill. They then let me experiment, learn, and grow on their dimes. They had the patience to see that I would deliver... even if how I delivered the results wasn't how they would have done it themselves.

I'm truly indebted to the team at Page Two. They've been an incredible partner in the creation of this book. Trena, Elana, Meghan, Jen, Lorraine, Adrineh, and the rest of the team have been a joy to work with. In particular, I can't give enough thanks to my editor (really, my collaborator), Amanda Lewis, who patiently prodded, pushed, suggested, sliced, diced, and shaped this book into a form that is wholly unrecognizable when compared to the bloated first draft I submitted to her (for which I'm very grateful).

I've been exceptionally fortunate to have a great business partner the past six years, my son, Alec. Everything I've achieved during this time is equally his success. He's produced over one thousand episodes of my show (and learned something about sales along the way). He's overseen the growth of my platform and our company. He's my chief strategist for our future growth and an indispensable partner in all that we do.

Lastly, as always, the most important member of my team is Vicky. None of this would have been possible without your encouragement, feedback, and support. Ours is one of the great love stories. And still a *lapin jour*.

NOTES

1   Mark Lindwall, Norbert Kriebel, Scott Santucci, Bradford J. Holmes, and Michael Shrum, "How Prepared Do Sales Reps Think They Are?" Forrester, February 11, 2013, forrester.com/report/How+Prepared+Do+Sales+Reps+Think+They+Are/-/E-RES104705.

2   This chart can be found at gartner.com/document/3994185.

3   Francesca Gino, "Let Your Workers Rebel," *Harvard Business Review*, October 24, 2016, hbr.org/2016/10/let-your-workers-rebel.

4   It's *How to Win Friends and Influence People*.

5   ASTD figures for 2014 are twenty billion dollars. Other surveys show the number around ten billion dollars (that's two grand per 4.5 million B2B sellers). From Sean Callahan, "The LinkedIn State of Sales Infographic: Some Numbers to Help You Hit Yours," LinkedIn Sales Blog, April 11, 2019, linkedin.com/business/sales/blog/b2b-sales/the-linkedin-state-of-sales-infographic-some-numbers-to-help-yo.

6   David Roberts, "Why Small Talk Is So Excruciating," Vox, December 30, 2019, vox.com/2015/7/7/8903123/small-talk.

7 Katherine Schaffstall, "Tom Hanks Jokes He Was 'Threatened' by Fan to Take Mister Rogers Seriously," Hollywood Reporter, November 26, 2019, hollywoodreporter.com/news/general-news/tom-hanks-playing-mister-rogers-jokes-he-was-threatened-by-fan-1258132/.

8 Brené Brown, *Dare to Lead* (Toronto: Random House Canada, 2018), Kindle.

9 Clayton Christensen (@claychristensen), Twitter, August 3, 2012, 11:28 a.m, twitter.com/claychristensen/status/231411154050748416?lang=en.

10 Tchiki Davis, "What Is Generosity (And How to Be a More Generous Person)," *Psychology Today*, February 4, 2019, psychology today.com/us/blog/click-here-happiness/201902/what-is-generosity-and-how-be-more-generous-person.

11 Diane Dormant, "A Trainer's Guide to Change Agentry," NSPI *Journal* 18, no. 3: 7–10. First published April 1979, onlinelibrary.wiley.com/doi/abs/10.1002/pfi.4180180306.

12 Timothy Hallinan, *Crashed (A Junior Bender Mystery)* (New York: Soho Press, 2012), Kindle.

ABOUT THE AUTHOR

 Hey, I'm Andy.

Many of you know me from my industry-leading sales podcasts, *Accelerate with Andy Paul* and *Sales Enablement with Andy Paul*. At the time of publication, I've produced over one thousand episodes of the absolute best conversations in sales, which millions of you have listened to (thank you for your support!).

Or perhaps you are one of the hundreds of thousands of sales professionals who follow my daily posts on LinkedIn. The conversations I have with you there are inspiring.

Or maybe you've read one of my other bestselling sales books.

So, you know that I believe that everything good in sales starts and ends with the individual salesperson. My mission over the past twenty years has been to elevate the individual seller.

Process, methodology and technology don't win deals; people do. People are the key differentiator. People buy from people. My whole career has been built on this understanding. It hasn't mattered whether I was selling computers to a small business, selling complex satellite communications systems to some of the largest enterprises in the world, or selling advisory services to a Fortune 500 firm. Everything I have achieved is based on the human-centered sales principles contained in this book.

You can achieve your goals too. I can help you. Follow me on LinkedIn to get my latest perspectives on work and life: linkedin.com/in/realandypaul.

Want More Andy?

Visit AndyPaul.com to learn how we can help you master the art of Selling In.

Join Andy's Community

Everyone is welcome. This is our free online community for human-centered sellers. We offer online courses on Selling In, community events, mentoring, exclusive content from Andy, and more! Go here to join: andypaul.com/community.

Transform Your Sales Results

Selling In positively transforms your sales results, the sales culture those results are built on, and how your customers experience buying from you. Bring Andy and his team in to assess, diagnose, and educate your sales team to elevate from Selling Out to Selling In. Go here to talk with Andy: andypaul.com/levelup.

Hire Andy to Speak to Your Sales Team

Andy's an educator, not a trainer. (If you need a trainer, we'll be happy to refer you.) In his fast-paced, entertaining, and educational presentations, either virtually or in person, Andy will help your sellers understand and embrace the practices and habits of Selling In. They'll thank you for it. Go here to talk with Andy: andypaul.com/getandy.

Build Your Personal Brand

It's a brand-new world out there. Sellers and sales leaders need to build their personal platform online. Increasingly, your brand is a key element of how you attract the interest of your buyers and differentiate yourself from competitors. We know how to do this. (Andy is the case study.) Go here to start the conversation: andypaul.com/mypersonalbrand.

LIKED THIS BOOK?
WRITE A REVIEW

YOU'VE FINISHED the book. You're excited. We're excited. Share the Selling In message with everyone you know.

Can I ask for a quick favor, while you're still buzzing about *Sell Without Selling Out*?

Help more sellers like you learn about this book by writing a short review online. Just a couple of lines about why you liked it would go far.

Books live and die based on word of mouth, and reviews at online retailers help a bunch. And I want *Sell Without Selling Out* to live a long, impactful life.

Thank you.

IT'S TIME TO STOP SELLING OUT.
AND START SELLING IN.

MAKE A BOLD STATEMENT. Buy a copy of *Sell Without Selling Out* for everyone on your revenue team today.

We love bulk orders! Let us create a customized, branded edition of *Sell Without Selling Out* for your company. We can do that in any format (physical, digital, or audio). And we can mix formats within an order to suit the learning style of your team. Let's talk about what will work best for your team.

Visit andypaul.com/bulkbuy.